PRAISE FOR *FINISH FIRST*

"In a no-nonsense style that reflects the energy and positivism he brings to every undertaking, Scott Hamilton makes his points clearly, concisely, and convincingly. *Finish First* will inspire you to turn every decision, every minute of every day, into one that moves you forward."

–GARY BETTMAN
Commissioner, National Hockey League

"Scott Hamilton explains—in the best way I have ever seen—the concept that failure is actually necessary in our lives in order for us to be winners. A smile came to my face as I read his words because I have lived them, and I understand. Now you will too!"

–DAN JANSEN
1994 Olympic Gold Medalist, speedskating

"I managed Scott Hamilton's business career during the twenty years he was a professional skater. I am also a very close friend. When I started working with Scott, he had already figured out how to be first in the world of skating. What I have seen up close and personal is how he has used those skills to become first in life. In many ways his post-skating career has been as difficult to navigate as his becoming an Olympic Champion!

"Scott took his competitive, athletic skills and applied them to his everyday life. In *Finish First* he shares many of his keys to a successful and meaningful life. That is what makes this book such a good read for anyone."

–BOB KAIN
Past president and Co-CEO of IMG

"Scott Hamilton makes no apologies for finishing first and outperforming his competitors, and neither should you. Competition makes us stronger, and winning allows us to reap the rewards that, in turn, enable us to give back to others and our communities so they can become stronger. I highly recommend this book for anyone looking for motivation to reach goals and who wants to stand on the winner's platform."

–TERRY J. LUNDGREN
Executive chairman, Macy*s, Inc.

"Scott Hamilton has overcome defeat, disappointment, cancer, brain tumors, and debilitating loss, has been overlooked and underappreciated, and yet has emerged as one of the greatest champions in the history of his sport. Scott is a winner both on and off the ice, and in *Finish First* he shows how you can be a winner too."

"Scott Hamilton has been a friend of mine for years. He's kind and humble and wildly talented. In this book he won't tell you what you want; he'll remind you about who you are. His message is simple: you'll finish first if you want it bad enough.

"Everyone has an opinion. Scott has a story. It's about love and grace and failing and trying again and winning. You're going to get clarity on your story as you read his. Buckle up. I know you're going to enjoy this book."

"Scott Hamilton's story is all about ignoring the doubters and living with purpose. You may be wondering if it's time to throw in the towel, but *Finish First* will challenge you to keep pushing forward. If you've got breath in your lungs, you still have time. It's never too late to start winning."

"Thank you for reminding me that slumps are but a choice and that finishing first is a way of life. I don't know where I'll end up down the road or what it will look like, but I'm determined to continue making choices and pushing myself in every aspect of my life to finish first!"

FINISH
FIRST

FINISH FIRST

WINNING CHANGES EVERYTHING

SCOTT HAMILTON
WITH ALLISON FALLON

W Publishing Group

An Imprint of Thomas Nelson

Published in Nashville, Tennessee, by W Publishing Group, an imprint of Thomas Nelson.

Authors are represented by Ambassador Literary Agency, Nashville, TN.

Thomas Nelson titles may be purchased in bulk for educational, business, fund-raising, or sales promotional use. For information, please e-mail SpecialMarkets@ThomasNelson.com.

Unless otherwise noted, Scripture quotations are taken from the Holy Bible, New International Version®, NIV®. © 1973, 1978, 1984, 2011 by Biblica, Inc.® Used by permission of Zondervan. All rights reserved worldwide.

Scripture quotations marked KJV are from the King James Version. Public domain.

Any Internet addresses, phone numbers, or company or product information printed in this book are offered as a resource and are not intended in any way to be or to imply an endorsement by Thomas Nelson, nor does Thomas Nelson vouch for the existence, content, or services of these sites, phone numbers, companies, or products beyond the life of this book.

ISBN 978-0-7852-1662-9 (TP)
ISBN 978-0-7852-1651-3 (eBook)

Library of Congress Cataloging-in-Publication Data

Names: Hamilton, Scott, 1958- author.
Title: Finish first : winning changes everything / Scott Hamilton with Allison Fallon.
Description: Nashville, Tennessee : W Publishing Group, [2018]
Identifiers: LCCN 2017040599 | ISBN 9780785216568 (hardcover)
Subjects: LCSH: Success. | Self-realization.
Classification: LCC BJ1611.2 .H29 2018 | DDC 650.1—dc23 LC record available at
  https://lccn.loc.gov/2017040599

Printed in the United States of America

19 20 21 22 23 LSC 10 9 8 7 6 5 4 3 2 1

This book is dedicated to everyone
who has suffered the pain of personal
failure, desires success, and is looking for
direction forward. I hope it gives you the
strength to rise up and finish first.

CONTENTS

FOREWORD

by Donald Miller

If you finish first, your friends may become jealous, your family might think you've gotten too big for your britches, and your competition might put a target on your back. So it's better to not compete. Better, that is, for your friends, your family, and your competition. But it's not better for you.

Many years ago I weighed 387 pounds, had little to no social life, could barely pay my rent, and spent countless hours feeling sorry for myself. There were many reasons for these things, but one of the main reasons was I felt an internal resistance to approaching life with a competitive mind-set. Why? Because there were too many people around who preferred me in the slow lane.

The reality is people are comfortable with you where you are. Your lack of success makes them feel safe and predictable because you serve as a point of reference for how much better their situation is than yours. Inside, you likely know if you start moving up, your sense of security in their ecosystem will be threatened. So you stay. But are you satisfied?

Losing as a means to survive socially is the stuff of a sad life. It's sad because the best thing that can happen to your friends, your family, and even your competition is for you to succeed. Yes, it may disrupt the ecosystem for a moment, but soon after you switch into a faster lane, the horns will stop honking, the middle fingers will descend, and people will begin to accept the new and improved you. And the friends worth keeping around will begin to improve their lives, too. Successful people set the pace for the rest of us.

I've known Scott Hamilton for years now. There is no better coach for anybody wanting to learn how to win. He's the kind of man who will pick somebody up when they've fallen on the ice. He knows that it's only on the 4,756th try that you stick the landing. When you imagine a winner, if you think of an angry coach disappointed in your performance or a cocky athlete holding a trophy in one arm and your girlfriend in the other, you've never met the right winner, the one who can help you finish first.

Scott's drive to finish first extends beyond his accomplishments as a gold-medal figure skater. He has three times beat cancer. He and his wife have taken on poverty in rural Haitian villages. He has transformed the lives of his coworkers, family, and friends by instilling in them a robust sense of hope and personal agency in the face of adversity.

What makes Scott unique is that he will go with you into your self-pity, comfort you as you cry, and bring understanding to your deepest places of shame. But he will not leave you there. He has learned that succumbing to the darkness is nobody's calling. This book reveals his belief that anybody can finish first and that competition is a food that nurtures lions.

In this book you will gain a willingness and even eagerness to compete. And competition is transformative.

In letting go of my fear to compete in life, I lost nearly 200 pounds, put multiple books on the *New York Times* bestsellers list, started a family, paid off my mother's house, started a mentoring organization, served on a president's advisory board, and built a multimillion-dollar business. My life got better when I realized my success was tied directly to the well-being of others and it wasn't going to hurt anybody, especially myself.

Share this book with your coworkers, your team, and your family. Agree with each other that competition is not bad and, when done with a generous spirit, brings out the best in all of us.

All this said, however, I can't end this foreword without being completely honest. I've still never finished first at anything. The highest any of my books have gotten on the bestsellers list is number 5. And while my company is a success, I have countless friends whose companies are bigger. I don't have a single trophy, and I've never even beaten my wife at checkers (she is ridiculously good at that stupid game), but I don't let it bother me. Why?

Because it's too fun to keep trying.

If a competitive spirit eludes you, may this book inspire you to compete and to try with all that is in you to finish first.

I'll race you.

INTRODUCTION

Winning does change everything. "I know you know that, but how?" you might ask.

Consider the classic story of David and Goliath. We all know the story of how the little shepherd boy who, even though he was too young and too small, stood up to a giant. And, against all odds, defeated him.

Then came opportunity. The Philistine army had a giant, and they wanted to resolve the war with one battle. Goliath, the Philistine, against Israel's best. Winner take all. Whoever lost would surrender and become slaves to the other. There wasn't one soldier in Israel's army who had the courage to stand up to this nine-and-a-half-foot giant. But then a small shepherd boy stood up and said that he would. He knew that the reward for winning this battle would change his life forever.

Even though his brothers scoffed and belittled him. Even though King Saul reminded David he was small and too young. David knew this was his chance and was willing to risk it all for a chance at a better life.

There aren't many people on the planet who don't know that story. What we don't talk about is what happened next.

After that victory, David's life became a photo negative of what it was before. Before he stood up to Goliath, he had the lowly job of looking after a few sheep with no real expectation of anything else. Okay, so the prophet Samuel knew that he would someday be king. But no one else in his life ever thought anything of David or his future. He went on to become the greatest king of his lifetime. And if you know Scripture, you know his life still has an impact today.

Could this be you?

Do you have the feeling that you have as many things going against you as David? That family, friends, and the people closest to you are always telling you why you can't do something? That your dreams are out of reach?

As children growing up, we have fantasies of winning the game. Or the award. Or the recognition that we know would make us feel good about ourselves.

As we grow up, we all would love to make straight As on our report cards. We know that would make our parents proud. And we would earn higher respect from our teachers. Those As build trust that make the next A easier to achieve. Academic success in high school makes it easier to get into a better college. Getting into a better college means getting a better job and everything that comes with it. Better opportunities mean better financial security. With more financial security comes a better lifestyle and a much better quality of life. With personal success, our children have more opportunities. And so on.

Making the choice to finish first will change the trajectory and quality of your life.

And will change EVERYTHING!

Here's how . . .

CHAPTER 1

WHY YOU AREN'T A WINNER—YET

Winning is not a sometime thing, it is an all the time thing. You don't do things right once in a while . . . you do them right all the time.

−VINCE LOMBARDI[1]

I have some bad news for you. You were not born a winner. You may have been told, somewhere along the way, that you were. Maybe your parents said you were "number one," no matter what you did. Or maybe a high school coach said all you needed to do to get the trophy was show up in the uniform and play a few innings. But those empty promises may have robbed you of your most victorious moments. They may have stolen the best you have to offer to yourself and to the world.

I was not born a winner, and neither were you. That might seem like a harsh thing to say, but it is actually the kindest, most important gift I can give you. Winning is not about getting an award or a medal or making a certain amount of money. Winning is about accessing all of your innate human potential. You cannot be born a winner. But you can become one.

What a tragedy that so many of us don't.

There might be a part of you that resists this, that wants to fight to keep the "winning" status you feel you've earned but haven't worked to achieve. And then there is another part of you, I'm convinced, that is whispering to you right now that you have so much untapped potential, skill and tenacity and talent that the world has yet to see. What will it take for you to unlock the champion trapped inside of you?

What will it take for you to choose to finish first?

My Unimpressive Beginnings

I wish you could have seen me at the beginning of my figure skating career. If you had been there, watching like a fly on the wall, you wouldn't have seen the person I am today. You would have seen someone else entirely. You would have seen a version of me that was more familiar with losing than he was with winning, who was terrified to make the sacrifices he knew it would take to become a winner, and who wondered if any of the work was even worth it. Winning has changed everything for me. It can change everything for you, too.

In the world of figure skating, I tell people that if you're a woman and you win, you're really good. If you're a man and you don't medal, you should probably think about doing something else. Still, for some reason, I kept skating even when I continually found myself in last place. That is a decision I will never fully understand, and yet I'm grateful I made it. Despite all the losing I endured, I knew there was a champion inside me yet to be revealed.

My first year at the Novice level—the lowest level for men's competitive figure skating to qualify for the US National Championships—I didn't even make it to the National Championships, let alone win a medal. My parents were always supportive and made continual sacrifices to keep me skating, without any expectation for success. But I realized at one point that if I was going to find my way to the winner's circle, I would have to take a different approach.

When I was thirteen years old, my parents decided to move me to a new training facility as a last-ditch effort to see if something would "click" for me there.

Wagon Wheel had a long track record of success. The facility wasn't cheap, and my parents weren't rich by any means. But they were relentlessly committed to helping me find my way in skating because they saw the health benefits it provided me in the midst of a world where the scales had been tipped against me.

I was an unwanted child, given up at birth by my biological mother and adopted at six weeks of age by my parents. I like to say that I remember it like it was yesterday. On top of that, I battled a rare and undiagnosed childhood illness that started at the age of four and came with all kinds of unpleasant symptoms. The worst of the symptoms was stunted growth, which left me shorter and smaller than all of my classmates. I remember being teased and bullied.

If you feel like you came into this life so far behind the starting line that you shouldn't even consider winning, you are not alone. Most people feel like the obstacles and challenges in their way are too big. They may even feel like they have been set up to fail before trying. We tend to become focused on what everyone else has that we don't—money, status, size, athleticism, access, relationships, and so on—and forget that the list of qualities it takes to be a winner has far more to do with what is inside of us than what is outside of us.

Most of my young life was consumed with hospital visits and doctor's appointments, and after years, we still didn't have any answers. I can only imagine how frustrated and discouraged my parents must have been, wondering if their son was ever going to be healthy and happy like the other kids. By the time I was nine years old, my parents were physically and emotionally depleted. Then, at the advice of our family physician, who insisted they take a morning off each week, my parents sent me to Saturday morning "learn to skate" classes at the brand-new skating rink at Bowling Green State University.

Like most skaters, my first steps on the ice were tentative and frightening. I spent most of that first morning holding on to the wall. I would find moments of bravery when I could let go for a brief time, but honestly, I held on more often than not. Over the next weeks I was able to get all the way around the ice without touching the wall. Soon I was skating as well as the healthy kids. Soon after that, I was skating as well as the best athletes in my grade. Self-esteem is a powerful force— and now I had it for the first time in my life.

I was small, my energy ran low, and I struggled with the effects of my undiagnosed illness, but skating offered me exactly what I needed. The cool, moist air helped with my lung condition, and the constant movement helped with my ability to digest food properly. The more I focused on skating, the less my body seemed to be in direct opposition to me. I started practicing and getting better. I began competing some and improving. Still, for all those first years of skating, I was underachieving.

You might be wondering, *So what if you were underachieving? Why should that even matter? If skating was helping with your symptoms, if it was bringing you joy, why should it matter if you win a gold medal?* My answer to those questions is that if I had never found a way to finish first in skating and the rest of my life, none of the other amazing, miraculous things I've experienced would have happened. As Vince Lombardi once said, "Winning isn't everything; it's the only thing."

What It Means to Finish First

To me, winning is not about holding a gold medal, losing the twenty pounds, getting a promotion, or seeing my name on a plaque. In fact, I won a gold medal in 1984, and it lived in a brown paper bag in my underwear drawer for years. I resisted the natural urge to worship the idol of that success. What I found to be more interesting was what I was becoming in the process of achieving the unthinkable.

When I talk about finishing first, I'm not talking just about beating your competitors. To finish first is to understand what you have to offer the world and then to be the best you can be at offering exactly that. It means understanding your life purpose and putting your whole heart into being the best at what you do. It means to break through your perceived limitations, overcome the barriers that stand in your way, and make the biggest impact in the world you are capable of making.

The general consensus of our culture seems to be that winning doesn't matter, that there's no point to trying hard because in the end, none of it matters. Instead of acknowledging who has won and who has lost, we hand out participation trophies and give everyone a ribbon before sending them home. Our fear of winning and losing has created an entire generation of entitled, apathetic, surefire losers. We haven't even stopped to consider the fact that losing might not hurt anyone. What if, by shielding people in this way, we're stealing the transformational power of both winning and losing in their lives?

The irony is that if you believe nothing matters in life, you will live a life that doesn't matter.

We have never been more confused as a culture about winning and losing—what it really takes and why it matters.

And yet I meet people every day who are hungry for more and desperate for something deeper, something better than the mediocre life they are living. The path to victory is precisely the thing that will open the door to the purpose they most crave.

Maybe to you it seems arrogant or selfish to think of yourself on a podium. You were trained to hold the door open for others, to be kind, thoughtful, sacrificial, and helpful. You were taught that the last would be first. Nothing is wrong with any of that. And as an Olympic athlete, I can say with confidence that the best way to help people—maybe even the only way to help anyone—is to start chipping away at the part of you that worries you don't have much to offer. Become someone who is worthy of winning, and you'll have a wider, greater impact than you ever dreamed possible.

In addition to this idea that winners are selfish and losers are the good guys, we also have the idea that winners and losers are preselected, and that doesn't feel fair. Yes, some of us are born with more resources than others, more access, more opportunities. But only one qualification makes someone more likely to win: they choose to win.

The number-one predictor for whether you will be a winner is if you decide to be one. It's a choice only you can make. And once you make it, nothing will be able to stop you.

The odds of me becoming an Olympic athlete were slim to none. Less than slim to none, actually. It was not even on my radar. It wasn't on my parents' radar, either. Yet my path to victory did something even more powerful than I could have predicted. Winning reshaped who I was as a person, helped to shape the world I live in, and even healed my physical body. Finishing first has opened doors for me to help others; it's given me a new lens through which to see my pain. It's helped me face the challenges of life with integrity and perseverance.

What if winning could do the same for you?

Are You Done Being a Loser?

When I moved to Wagon Wheel in 1972, my skating immediately began to improve. I was surrounded by people who were better skaters than I was and had access to more experienced coaches. Everything and everyone began calling me to a higher standard. My work ethic improved, and I started to see myself as being able to hold my own with my competition. I even made it to the National Championships that year.

The problem was, at Nationals, I fell five times and came in dead last. Dead. Last. Talk about losing. At least when I lose, I go all the way. Of all the losers, I proved to be the best.

Looking back, I can't help but think about how important all of this losing was in terms of preparing me for my future success. This is something few people talk about—how much losing really goes into winning. If there were a recipe for winning, losing would be a main ingredient. Just when you think you've added too much, add some more.

You'll be hard-pressed to find a champion who hasn't had more than an average amount of losing in his or her story—myself included. And yet I meet people all the time who worry that they've been disqualified from winning because they've lost so many times. Are you kidding? Losing is your greatest asset, and I'll talk more about that in chapter 8. When I meet people who aren't losing enough, I immediately wonder why they haven't taken more risks, who has been insulating them from the possibility of failure, and what potential they still have hidden inside of them.

Of course losing is embarrassing. It's humiliating. But it also fuels us.

It changes us. It humbles us. And it plants in us the character we need to sustain the long-term kind of achievement we crave. If you're sick of losing, you're in the right place. What I'm about to share with you is a way to live that can help you become the winner you may have only dreamed you could one day be.

When I think about what happened that year at Nationals, all I can say is that I choked. It was my shot, and I blew it. You've probably had a moment like this, a moment where none of your excuses held up anymore and you knew that losing could only be your own fault. That was me at the end of Nationals that year. And as I sat in the embarrassment of that moment, I realized something important: I didn't want to be a loser anymore.

In fact, there was a specific moment I made this decision. It was after the competition, and I was at a victory party for Gordie McKellen, the men's national champion of the year. We were all relaxing, having a good time. At one point one of the other skaters my age looked over at me.

"Hey, go grab me a beer," he said, pointing to the open cooler.

"Why don't you go grab your own beer?" I asked, a little confused about why he was bothering me for something he was perfectly capable of doing himself. He looked back at me and then back at the beer and then back at me.

"Because you have nothing to lose. I do," he said.

Suddenly I got it. Never have I felt the weight of losing so heavily, and never had it been more clear to me. I was over this. I was done being a loser. I didn't care what it took or how much it cost me. I was ready to be the kind of person worthy of the position I desired. I was ready to do the work. I was ready to change from the inside out. I was ready to become a winner. What I didn't know at that point was that I wasn't done losing yet.

Your Path to Victory

When I think back on my move to Wagon Wheel, I realize that this was the first big shift for me in my competitive career and that it would never have happened if I had started out even moderately successful. If I had made it to Nationals the year that I didn't, for example, my parents never would have invested the resources for me to go to Wagon Wheel. I would have just stayed where I was. Have you ever stopped for a minute to think about how many things had to go wrong in your life for you to end up exactly where you are?

This is important because a lot of people wonder why the United States isn't as competitive in skating as it used to be. And I believe it's because we've lowered the bar as far as who goes to the National Championships. The best possible thing that could have happened to me was not making it. It changed the way I approached my skating and my commitment to get better. By allowing anyone who wants to compete to go to Nationals, we are robbing all skaters of developing that burning desire to win.

I say this to point out that no matter where you are today, this is your path to victory. It will be paved with so much disappointment, so much failure. You will question yourself and question your path. This is part of the process.

I often meet people who have lists of reasons why they will never be successful. They list their failures, their critics, and their setbacks. They talk to me about how they've wasted time. They tell me it's too late. And I tell them the same thing: The path to victory is the path you're on. It becomes a path to victory the moment you decide it does. You think that doing what it takes to win will be miserable, but the real misery comes when you lose because you weren't willing to do the simple things it takes to become a champion.

Honestly, I'm grateful for all of my losing. Without that experience, I wouldn't have any idea why it matters so much to be a winner. And I wouldn't know any of what I'm about to tell you—about how you can become the winner you wondered if it was even possible for you to be.

CHAPTER 2

KNOW YOUR PURPOSE

The purpose of life is not to be happy—but to
matter, to be productive, to be useful, to have it
make some difference that you lived at all.

–LEO ROSTEN[1]

What were you made to do that you aren't doing?
You get a glimpse into your purpose by paying
attention to the things you love, what you're good at, and where
opportunities are open for you. When you're a skater, you
skate. When you're a writer, you write. When you're a teacher,
you teach. And you do those things with everything you have
because when your purpose presents itself, you owe it to yourself to follow through.

I get excited by the kind of person I know you will become
when you give up your excuses and start uncovering what
you've been capable of all this time. I get excited by the kind of

impact you will be able to have when you stop playing small, when you get out of your own way, when you are ready to be done holding back and to become all you were made to be. I get excited by inspiring every individual I meet to access his or her great potential so that the world doesn't miss what he or she brings to the table. This is what finishing first is about for me. It's not about proving yourself or beating your competitors but about accessing your deep purpose.

What is your unique purpose? Do you know? If you do know, have you taken any time to stop and make sure you're doing what you were put here to do?

My faith tells me that everything is meaningful, that nothing happens by accident. You are here for a reason. If you don't know that reason yet, you are probably struggling and miserable.

What You Really Want

You hear life coaches and inspirational gurus say all the time, "Nothing is out of your reach," but I have a problem with that statement. It's not that I disagree. I don't. It's just that too many of us move through the world with a sense of entitlement, thinking we should be able to have whatever we want, whenever we want it, and that it should be handed to us on a silver platter without us having to pay for it. What I've learned over time is that it's mostly unhelpful to tell people that they can have whatever they want because most of us have no idea what we truly want. What we think we want isn't what we want at all, and what we really want is to fulfill our purpose.

We all have a unique purpose. Exodus 9:16 says, "But I have raised you up for this very purpose, that I might show you my power and that my name might be proclaimed in all the earth." There is a greater purpose at work than your personal happiness or satisfying your ego. Sometimes we resist our purpose because it doesn't seem convenient or because it won't look cool on Instagram. But you can't argue against your purpose. Michael Jordan, although one of the best basketball players of all time, will never do a backflip on ice skates. And I will never dunk a basketball.

Purpose is the difference between a pipe dream and a goal worth all the sacrifice it will take to get it. Purpose is the difference between your ego telling you to do something and God telling you to do it. Purpose is the difference between waiting around for your big break and understanding what it actually takes to make you a champion. Each of us was put here with a unique and specific purpose, and that purpose will drive us toward our goal if we can determine what it is.

For most people, the answer comes to mind right away. But if you're having trouble, my guess is that it's because your purpose is being drowned by the sound of the critics in the back of your mind, telling you that you're too tall or too short or that you don't have the background or the training or the pedigree to do what you were made to do. Let me be the first to say that if you were made to do something, none of those qualifications matter. I'm a prime example of this.

Have you seen the popular movie *Rudy*, about the Notre Dame football player Rudy Ruettiger? It's an amazing story and an another perfect example of what I'm talking about. Rudy was told he was too small to play football, that he was not smart enough, that he'd never make it on the team. At first glance, you might say Rudy's critics were right. He was too small to play football. He was only five foot six, nearly a foot shorter than some of his teammates, and only 165 pounds. But Rudy wasn't willing to accept this as his final answer. He knew his purpose was to play Notre Dame football.

So he chipped away at his weaknesses. Little by little. One by one. He put in the work—more work than most of his teammates—and finally earned his way onto the field. He was never going to be the best player. But that didn't matter. Nothing was going to stop Rudy from achieving his goal. Not his critics, not his brothers, not his dad, not even his coach.

Rudy's goal wasn't to become the greatest player of all time. His goal was to prove to himself that with heart and dedication, you can really achieve anything you set out to do. And Rudy proved to all of us that when you know your purpose, there are no limits to what the human spirit can achieve.

Sometimes our purpose is obvious. Michael Phelps was built to be a swimmer. Michael Jordan was built to be a basketball player. Sometimes our purpose is less obvious. Was I built to be an ice skater? Not necessarily. But I wasn't willing to give up. And neither was Rudy. What we shared was a deep knowledge that nothing could get in the way of us achieving our purpose on this planet. If you know your purpose, nothing can stop you, either.

If you don't know your purpose, here are some questions to ask yourself. What do you *love* to do? When are you happiest, most excited, and most engaged in what you're doing? What are you gifted to do? And how can you turn that into something meaningful for your life and for the world?

Some people argue that they don't have a gift or that the only thing they love to do is sit around and hang out with their friends. My pushback to them is always to dig a little deeper.

Are you naturally good at telling and understanding stories? Pay attention to that. Are you seven feet tall? That's significant. Are you naturally good with children? That's a gift. Lean into it. If we can stop for a moment and be quiet, we can hear through the noise of the world and take stock of our natural gifts and capabilities. There, we find our great purpose.

Try Something New

Maybe you haven't discovered your unique purpose yet. Or maybe you're really close, but you need to make the smallest shift to the right or to the left. Maybe your purpose is down a completely different path than the one you've been walking, or maybe it's right in front of you or behind you and you just need a new way to look at it.

If what you have been doing isn't working or isn't working as well as you want it to, or if you're just not having fun, consider the option that it might be time to try something new.

My friend Sterling Ball (you may know him if you've purchased his Ernie Ball guitar strings) is a legendary figure in the music world—an award-winning bass designer, industry leader, and accomplished bass player who performs with his friends Albert Lee, Steve Lukather, and Steve Morse. If you're a guitar player, you know who this man is because his reputation precedes him.

But despite Sterling's obvious success in the world of music, there came a point when he realized there was something else he wanted to do that had nothing to do with music. It was something with which he had very little experience but something he was passionate about. He wanted to enter the world of competition barbecue.

As a newcomer to the industry, he had a lack of experience going against him. But he did his research. And he knew the world of barbecue was massively underserved. In fact, he had two things to bring to the table that he knew were missing. One, he could apply his marketing skills to an industry that wasn't utilizing broad marketing. Two, he saw that he could leverage his passion for cooking in a unique way to an industry that needed more innovation.

To try something new, we have to be willing to check our egos at the door. We have to move out from under what is comfortable and be willing to take the risk of being bad at something, or making fools of ourselves, or letting people ask those questions like, "Barbecue? Why barbecue?" When they ask that, we can say, "Because it's fun!"

The results of his commitment and participation came quickly. Within months of coming on the scene, Sterling had secured the American Royal Invitational award, one of the most prestigious awards in barbecue. Now he's ranked as one of the top twenty-five most influential people in barbecue. Not to mention, in his spare time, he developed a line of championship rubs. He's changing the world one delicious bite at a time. All because he was willing to try something new.

We all have something to offer. And that's really what finishing first is about at the end of the day—making sure we're offering exactly what we have to offer. No more, no less.

Even when things aren't going exactly your way, when it seems like you are the least likely candidate for success, when it seems like everybody else is getting there while you're lagging behind, remember your purpose. Remember to check your ego at the door. Remember that if you're willing to put in the work, you'll have a firm foundation of character to stand on when you reach your victory. There is no way this world will miss what you have to give it.

Our family just came back from Disney World, and I spent some time while I was in the park just sitting. Looking at people. Paying attention.

As I looked around at the crowds of people, I found myself thinking about how every person in that park has an incredible story to tell. You have an incredible story to tell. Some nugget of wisdom to share. Some gift that the world needs you to give. There were so many people in the park that we had friends there from Nashville and we didn't bump into any of them all week. Imagine the crowds! And within those crowds were hundreds of thousands of beautiful stories, beautiful lives, undiscovered talents and gifts and successes.

Who of us doesn't want to look back on our days here on this planet and feel that we fulfilled our purpose? That we didn't take a pass on the gifts buried deep inside of us? If each of us decided today that we were going to be a little more productive, a little more sacrificial, a little more selfless, a little more kind, a little more forgiving, and a little more hard working, the planet would change in an instant. That's the kind of victory I'm pulling for. That's what it would look like for us to finish first.

One of my favorite verses in the Bible, Romans 8:28, says, "And we know that in all things God works for the good of those who love Him, and who have been called according to His purpose." If you want to know your purpose, look to God, who promises He will reveal it to you. It's always in His timing. When we fix our eyes on Him, He takes even the worst parts of our story and uses them for His greater good, His greater glory. It doesn't matter how far behind the starting line you think you are. You are here to reflect His goodness and grace.

CHAPTER 3

BREAK THE PATTERN
OF LOSING

The battle of life is, in most cases, fought uphill;
and to win it without a struggle were perhaps to
win it without honor. If there were no difficulties
there would be no success; if there were nothing to
struggle for, there would be nothing to be achieved.

—SAMUEL SMILES, AUTHOR AND POLITICIAN[1]

If I had to write a dating profile for myself—and I was being honest—it would read, "Short, bald, half-neutered, chemoed, radiated, retired male figure skater of unknown ethnic origin seeks a beautiful, intelligent woman for long walks, laughter, and an interest in my hobby of collecting life-threatening illnesses." And yet, somehow, I am married to a beautiful, incredible woman who loves me. I have four great kids and an Olympic gold medal (which, you'll be happy to know, is no longer hidden in my sock drawer—it's in the World Figure Skating Museum and Hall of Fame in Colorado Springs, in case you want to go look at it).

If that's not an advertisement for how we are not defined by our challenges, I don't know what is. And yet, for many of us, our pattern of losing gets in the way of our great potential before we even give winning a chance.

Losing is so much more familiar to us than winning. In fact, for most of us, I think losing is all we know. It's easier. It's comfortable. Very little is expected of those who lose. And the more we lose, the more we expect to lose, which sets us up for more losing. When you expect something to happen, for the most part, it happens. No wonder you keep losing—you see yourself as someone who constantly loses!

Can you relate to this? No matter how hard you work, no matter how many diet programs you try, no matter how many hours you put in at the office, you keep falling short. After all of that effort and all of the negative results over and over again, of course you would lose motivation to keep trying. That mentality is only natural. But what if you could move beyond what is "natural" to something supernatural? What if you could defy all odds to achieve your greatest, most hidden potential?

When it came to breaking my own pattern of losing, it didn't happen overnight. After my devastating loss at Nationals, I made the firm decision that things were going to be different for me from then on out. I was never going to be in last place again. But when I arrived at Nationals the following year, with all of my renewed determination, I finished ninth. Out of ten. The year after that, I moved up to Junior level, figuring, what's the worst that could happen? I went with a double axel in my arsenal, convinced that it was going to be my chance to move up the ranks. When it came time, I gave what felt like a solid performance. I came in seventh. Of nine.

The pattern of losing can be broken, but not without a serious shift in mentality and focus. Without the right train of thought, you are doomed to be stuck in your losing pattern forever. But the smallest shift can have a seismic impact. With a few small perspective changes, you might be able to access the winner lying asleep deep within you.

Did you know that Oprah Winfrey was fired from her first television job? This was years before becoming the first black woman to host a television program in Nashville, Tennessee. What changed for Oprah? What shifted that helped her move from such a terrible loss to become the legendary figure she is today? What if Oprah had taken her pattern of losing as a sign that she wasn't meant to be on television in the first place?

What about Michael Jordan, who admits to losing three hundred games in his career? What if Jordan had let his pattern of losing define who he was? What if he had gotten stuck in that pattern of losing so that he never became a winner?

Did you know Dick Cheney dropped out of college only later to become the forty-sixth vice president of the United States? What shifted for Cheney that helped him leverage his losses and get out of his pattern of losing?

What would the world be like if these revolutionary figures hadn't broken their patterns of losing? What would we have missed, as a culture, if they hadn't moved past the obvious barriers in front of them and defied all odds to win?

When life circumstances spin out of your control, when it seems like the entire world is conspiring against you to keep you losing over and over again, you have two choices. You can accept what is. That is an understandable choice. An ordinary path. A natural way of thinking about things. Or you can choose a different route. The other way is not natural at all. It's far more challenging. It will take your breath away. It will also change your whole life. It will change the whole world.

Are you ready?

Running Out of Time

Shortly after I finished seventh out of nine at Nationals, my parents sat me down and told me that things were about to change. My mom was sick, they said, and we were running out of money. I had one year left in skating. Suddenly everything that had mattered so much before didn't matter anymore. I wasn't interested in protecting myself from failure or in messing around or wasting more time. There wasn't enough time to be wasting.

Few things shake you out of your pattern of losing like tragedy.

As I sat there and let the words they were saying sink in, I thought about how unfair it was that she was the one who was sick. She was such a special person. She had always believed in me, no matter what. She had sacrificed everything to make sure I could keep skating. All of a sudden I realized how selfish it had been for me to be underachieving the way I was. There wasn't much time left for me to prove I was worth all of the sacrifices she had made. This was the wake-up call I needed.

It's interesting how this happens—how when life takes a left turn we didn't expect, we suddenly discover the strength, resilience, and power that has been inside us all along. Maybe there is a way for us to get this wake-up call without having to get the "wake-up call," if you know what I mean.

As soon as I made the decision to get my act together, things started falling into place. This is so amazing to me about how God works. All He needs is our willingness, and He does the rest; 2 Samuel 22:33 says, "God is my strength and power: and he maketh my way perfect" (KJV).

When I look back over how my life has unfolded, I'm convinced God is the one who has made my way perfect. All I offered was a willingness to go wherever He called me to go.

Shortly after the news came about my mom, the coach I had been working with retired. This meant I inherited a new coach, who was more strict than any coach I had worked with previously. In fact, he made it clear that if he was going to coach me, I would need to take it to the next level. It wasn't that I wasn't working hard. It's just that I knew I had more to give. This is the thing with human potential. We have far more to offer than we tend to realize we do.

My new coach only worked with champions, and even though I wasn't there yet, I had to start acting like I was. He was a taskmaster. Unforgiving. No student of his was going to be mediocre. I was no exception.

In addition to him expecting more of me as a skater, I also started expecting more of myself. I began to rise to the occasion for maybe the first time in my career. Suddenly it felt like time was pressing and that if I didn't take advantage of what was in front me, I might miss my chance completely. There was a tangible, noticeable shift in me that year.

I'll let you in on a little secret. There's a way to train that gets you results, and there's a way to train that looks like you're working hard but won't get you to the promised land of finishing first. Actually, my guess is that this isn't much of a secret for you. We all have our ways of cutting corners creatively so that no one will realize we aren't bringing our best selves to the table. For me, I would work sections of my program without going through the whole thing from start to finish. I did just enough so no one could accuse me of slacking—but I knew.

As soon as I realized that running my programs all the way through would better prepare me for competition and, in fact, have a measurable impact on my performance, I became more intentional about doing it that way. Every time. It was harder, took more energy, and left me more tired at the end of practice, but now I was committed to doing it. I was going to do whatever it took.

A world-renowned Russian coach came up to me once

and said, "So you run your programs all the way through every day?" I nodded. She said, "I tried to get my skaters to do that, but they got so tired." Yes. This is exactly the point. We haven't really given all we have to give until we've given all we have to give, until we finish practice with nothing left in our tank.

Two weeks before Nationals, I starting landing my first triple. Who was this person who was suddenly acting like a winner? Something had changed. And for the first time ever, it felt like maybe the pattern of losing had been broken. I wasn't a loser anymore. I wasn't on the winner's podium yet, but somehow, some way, I started to believe that maybe I could be.

When I travel and speak, I meet people all the time—usually folks in their fifties or sixties—who feel like they're running out of time. In fact, feeling like you're running out of time might just be the encouragement you need to get started. It's much easier when you're young and healthy to put off the things that matter to you most. You think you'll have endless time to make your life count. Then something shifts, and you realize there is no such thing as endless time. What a blessing.

It's never too late to get started, no matter how late in life you choose to do it. Finishing first has immediate benefits. No matter what your age—how old or how young—it's time to stop thinking that time is going to last forever. This one life is the only life we get. This short amount of time is the only time we have. What will it take for us to see ourselves as the winners we are? What will it take for us to uncover our potential?

The Hunger to Win

I know you want to be a person of value. You want to be the kind of person others think of when they consider who they want on their teams. You want to have the kind of character that sets an example for everyone else in the room. But how do you go from someone who is constantly losing to someone worthy of the title "winner"? How do you gain the character, integrity, and work ethic it takes to withstand long-term success?

I talked to my friend Mike Eruzione on the phone recently. Mike was the captain of the 1980 US Olympic hockey team—a team that beat the unbeatable Soviet national team to win the gold. This was a feat that would later be referred to as the "Miracle on Ice." As I was telling Mike about this book, I asked him if he had any thoughts to share about becoming a winner.

He said, "Most people make winning too complicated. This is not about magic fairy dust . . . It just comes back to a basic believing in yourself."

Mike is right, and his advice is a thread that ties together thousands of stories of people who have become champions despite the odds. People who end up winning do so because they decide they're going to do it. They have a hunger. They decide that they won't quit—that they won't allow anyone to take from them the thing they most want. They have made up their minds that they deserve it as much as anyone else. If you're questioning whether you deserve to win, let me ask you this: Why not you? If you don't win, it's going to be someone else.

Even if you think you don't have what it takes to win, you can decide that you do. Next time you look in the mirror and think about how you don't have the build, don't have the skills, or don't have the opportunities, remember me. Take one look at me. I was an unwanted child, sick for most of my early life. My parents had limited income and weren't into athletics. They didn't always know the exact clinics I needed to attend or have connections to the best coaching. We lived in a small town and had limited access to resources.

I came from limited financial means, so paying a high price for coaching was out of the question. My parents encouraged me to keep going out there, keep skating—but none of us knew what we were doing. The ingredients do not add up to me going to two Olympic Games and going undefeated for four years in between. That position should have belonged to someone else, to someone born into an athletic family, in a big city, with great coaching and money to buy the best equipment—right?

This is proof that there is only one irreplaceable ingredient in the recipe of success: hunger. How much do you want it?

I meet people every day who want to win, but they don't necessarily say those words. Instead, they say things like, "I'm bored with my life" or "I feel like I could do more." They talk about being tired of the "grind" at work, having low energy, or wishing life were more exciting. They tell me about someone they love, something they've lost, or how life hasn't gone the way they planned. They wish they had the power to make a change. I just look at them and tell them they've got it—the hunger to win.

I can only imagine that there is something on your mind right now, something you want that you haven't been able to get. I'm here to tell you that you can have it. First you have to believe you're worthy of winning.

A winning mind-set is one that says, "I won't be denied. I won't allow myself to be taken off this path." It's a matter of deciding that you can't be talked out of a victory that is yours, no matter how many unforeseen circumstances try to derail you. You can accept the facts of your situation and also decide you aren't going to let them hold you back anymore.

Here's something to think about: When it comes to the end of your life, what do you want people to say about you? What words do you want spoken at your funeral? Do you want people to say that you really put yourself out there, gave it your best shot? Or do you want people to say that you listened to your critics, let fear hold you back, and could have done more? Most of us settle for the latter.

We're all dealt a different hand in this life. I don't know what hand you were dealt. But I know that the only thing we can do with our hand is play it—no bluffing. You can make the choice. You can either waste the opportunities you've been given, waste away in your regrets and failures, waste your gifts, waste your time and energy and effort, and wait for your participation ribbon. Or you can choose to finish first.

Which will you choose?

Real Competition Elevates Everyone

In those early days when I was training at Wagon Wheel, I was surrounded by some of the most phenomenal athletes in the world.

Obviously, I was the worst skater there. So why, after watching what the other skaters could do, didn't I feel like, "There's no way I'll ever be able to amount to anything"? Instead, being there inspired me to believe I could do so much more than I was doing. Even though I wasn't living up to my full potential, I knew I could be. If they could do it, I thought to myself, why couldn't I? This is what winning does. Watching others succeed gave me permission to fantasize about my own version of finishing first.

This is why it's so important for us to win according to our purpose. This isn't just about feeding our egos. It's about creating a world where the expectation is that you have much more to offer. You are capable of more than you're giving. I want my kids to grow up in this kind of world, not a watered-down world.

Part of me wonders, in a world that seems so divided and divisive, if we're really at odds with one another or if we're just feeling entitled and lazy. Maybe we're just so bored with our comfortable lives that we have to find something to fill our time. As humans, we are wired for challenge, so if we don't challenge ourselves, we'll find petty drama and arguments to keep us busy. Spend time around people who are truly working to bring the best version of themselves to the world, and my guess is that we won't feel much like arguing anymore.

You become like the people with whom you spend the most time. So it should be no surprise that spending time with people who beat me constantly didn't deter me from finishing first. Instead, it helped me access my own will to win. Why is it that we get so caught up with thinking that beating someone is bad for them? What if winning is the kindest, bravest, most helpful thing you can do?

Healthy competition teaches us. It doesn't hold us back. It pushes us forward. When we bring our best to the competition, it challenges everyone to dig deep and discover their hidden talents, their buried tenacity, their untapped skill. You were put on this Earth to do something amazing. Something nobody else can do. The only way you can do that thing is to tap into your deepest power, your greatest potential. Far too many of us are missing it because we're worried about making a way for someone else.

Act Like a Winner

When I made it to the Junior level at Nationals that next year, I was armed with my first triple jump. Things had shifted for me, and it showed. I carried myself differently, acted differently, and felt differently about myself. Honestly, I felt like a different person. The shift that had taken place inside of me showed on the outside. People looked at me differently.

They started to take me seriously, the way they did the other winners.

I skated a strong short program and finished that performance higher on the scoreboard than I ever had—third. Going into the long program, I was feeling good. I was ready to unleash my triple jump. My coach warned me not to practice the triple in warm-up in case I didn't have it but told me that if I was feeling ready during the performance, I could go for it. I took his advice and practiced the double. Then, when I came out on the ice to perform the long program, I was on fire. I felt firm and grounded and ready for anything.

I got through the first few jumps in my program without any glitches, which built up my confidence. Without thinking too much, I skated as fast as I could down the ice and readied myself for the jump. I mentally checked my form and alignment, set it up, and let it go. For what seemed like an eternity, I hung in the air. Then, without any fanfare, I felt my skates hit the ice. I landed it! The crowd cheered, and I knew what this meant. This was a turning point for me. I wasn't in the losing circle anymore.

For the first time, I started to feel like maybe I belonged in the winner's circle. I had something to offer. When you start to act like a winner, you feel like a winner. When you start to feel like a winner, you act like a winner. The pattern of losing has been broken. This isn't a place for "those other people," it's a place for you. And when you begin to take yourself seriously like this, other people begin to take you seriously, too.

I won the Junior level at Nationals that year and left feeling like a million bucks.

Not only had I skated to my greatest potential and gotten the trophy to show for it, but I also felt like I had honored my mom's sacrifice to keep me in skating. I was making her proud, and I knew that this was the kind of performance of which I could be personally proud. An entire world of opportunity was opening in front of me. There was only one problem. My parents had already warned me: this was my last year of skating.

Believe You Are Worthy of Winning

What does a diamond look like when it comes out of the ground? It needs some polishing, some chiseling, and some attention and care. It might not seem like much at first, but with some work, it becomes something of incredible value. You are a diamond. You may need some polishing. Some chiseling. But underneath your weaknesses and flaws, you can really shine.

Take a look at the people standing where you want to stand. What does that manager, leader, or champion have that you don't have? You can acquire those same skills and abilities. If they seem more worthy than you, it's only because they've put in the time and work. We're all like diamonds. You can become precious. You can reveal your priceless qualities. You must find your greatest opportunity for contribution in the world.

If you're wondering if you have the qualities and characteristics of a person capable of finishing first, let me tell you how you can know. You are willing to do whatever it takes to get the qualities you need to succeed at fulfilling your purpose. This will make you worthy of facing the next challenge as it comes—and it will.

Something amazing happens when you make yourself worthy of winning. The support you need to win starts coming to you. The coaches, the education, the training, the resources. Everything you need begins to come to you.

When I look back and think about how that year was supposed to be my last in skating, I can't believe the path that opened for me instead. If I had come in seventh that year at Nationals, I wouldn't have caught the eye of a coach who had a sponsor for me that would keep me on the rink for another year. I wouldn't have any of the things I enjoy in my life now— financial stability, a wife who loves me, and four amazing children.

Even if I had attained my greatest result in skating—if I had come in fourth—I never would have caught the attention of the coaches and sponsors who kept me on the ice. But I didn't come in seventh. Or fourth. I came in first. Finishing first changes everything.

Thank God I woke up to the truth about myself when I did.

Thank God I made the decision to be a winner that year—to submit to my coaches, to submit to the process, to begin acting like the winner I was.

Thank God I decided to go all the way. What will you choose?

CHAPTER 4

COMMIT TO THE LONG HAUL

Success is the sum of small efforts
repeated day in, and day out.

–ROBERT COLLIER[1]

Several months ago I had the opportunity to test drive a Tesla. What I learned was that there's this setting on the dashboard called *Ludicrous Speed*. Literally. You push a little button that says "Ludicrous," and the car asks you, "Would you like to go Ludicrous Speed?" If you say yes, you can go from 0 to 60 in 2.2 seconds. It's thrilling. And at the same time it feels a little bit like you are going to lose your lunch.

I enjoyed driving the Tesla as much as anybody would, but it made me think. In a world driven by modern conveniences, a major obstacle getting in the way of wannabes becoming champions is that they expect the process to be fast and easy. Like a Tesla. After all, everything in the world is fast and easy. Here's the problem: If you expect winning to be fast and easy, you'll never access your winning potential. In fact, if you imagine that there is a button to get you down the road at ludicrous speed, you'll miss the long, excruciating, and unforgiving road that actually gets you there.

It's a journey—a long one, where you don't always know the outcome when you get started. But if you can learn to find joy in the journey, you can't go wrong. The whole point is that our life is built one brick at a time.

If you want to learn how to play the piano, you have to start by learning the notes in a scale. You learn one note at a time. Have you listened to someone learning to play the piano recently? They don't start by playing melodies. They start by plunking one key at a time. It doesn't sound all that great, but if you have little ones who are learning to play, you celebrate those tiny successes so that they keep playing. Eventually they are able to put those notes together into something that vaguely resembles music. It just takes a while.

If you want to learn to be an ice skater, you have to start by putting on skates and stepping onto the ice. If I were going to teach you to skate—and let's say you've ice skated a handful of times before in your life, on public rinks, around in circles—I wouldn't have you doing triple axels on your first practice. I'd start by having you get comfortable moving around on the ice. Baby steps.

We have to think of this as an exercise of building. You're

building a house. Building a city. Rome wasn't built in a day. Neither will your success be.

A friend of mine had a hard time in accounting class remembering which way to enter the credits and debits when building a spreadsheet, so he came up with a small trick to help him remember. It went like this: debit toward the window, credit toward the door. In other words, if he could imagine himself in the classroom where his accounting class took place, all he had to do was enter the debit toward the window and the credit toward the door. It's catchy, easy to remember, and, at fifty years old, he still jokes about it.

These are the tactics and small steps we celebrate in young children when they're learning to do something new, and yet we don't give ourselves permission to do the same thing. We underplay our small wins, downplay them, act like they aren't a big deal, when really these are the building blocks of the success we so crave. Without them, we have nothing.

There is no such thing as a big win without a thousand small victories that come before it. We're building a house. You can't do it with a single brick. You need thousands of them. Each brick stacked on top of another.

Building the Muscles of Maturity

I wish I could say that after winning Nationals for the first time, everything changed for me. But nothing changes that quickly. Instead, shortly after that taste of winning, I went back to my losing ways. The next year—my first senior year at Nationals—I came in ninth, which was upsetting. That was not supposed to be how the story went. And yet it went that way. I didn't have what it took to hold on to the win.

At the time, the whole thing felt confusing to me. Maybe you can relate. A door of opportunity opens—a new job, a promotion, a connection to someone in your industry—and you step into the opportunity for a moment, but days or weeks later, you blow it. You stay out late with friends instead of finishing your work. You sleep past your alarm and show up late. Few things in life are more frustrating than realizing you have made it to the winner's circle but you don't have what it takes to stay there.

This is what happened to me the year after my Junior level win at Nationals. I had what I like to call the "trifecta of immaturity." First, I was being sponsored, which meant that for one of the first times in my life, I didn't have to worry about money. Second, I turned eighteen. And, third, I got my own apartment. So I went from having relatively no freedom and no responsibility to having tons of freedom and tons of responsibility. And like so many young people today, I didn't have the character to sustain any of it.

I was free to do whatever I wanted, and I did. I was mostly committed but not completely. I showed up for practice most of the time but not all of the time. Part of me felt like since I was now a "winner," I didn't have to work quite as hard. The title should just be handed to me.

It's amazing how easy it is to get here when we treat our "wins" as destinations rather than as small stops on the journey. Titles aren't passed down through generations. Winning is never guaranteed. It's given to those who fight the hardest, who decide not to give up, and who know that finishing first has more to do with commitment and dedication than it does with an overinflated ego. A winning life, a winning attitude is built over a very long period of time.

For a long time, I beat myself up for how I acted in those early days.

Now, looking back, I realize it was just a matter of immaturity, evidence that I had more work to do. I needed more consistency and repetition. Even though I grabbed that one small win, I didn't have the strength and stamina to hold on to it. I'll address this more in the later chapters of this book, but it's like any muscle you build. There's going to be pain attached to it—not to mention, it takes a long time to build character and accountability. It doesn't happen at ludicrous speed.

A muscle comes in many shapes and sizes. As you fight your way to become a champion, you'll need to build your mental muscles, your spiritual muscles, your emotional muscles, and your physical muscles. Every challenge that comes your way is another opportunity to build these muscles.

Honestly, I shouldn't have even made it out of Sectionals that year, but by some miracle, I did. And I started to notice that winning wasn't something that happens to you but something you build, something you fight for, a way of living that dictates everything about how you do your life.

Stress Breeds Strength

There's a slim chance you might be able to make a bit of success happen overnight—either because of talent or just luck. But luck is not a firm foundation. I can list a dozen truly talented people who, despite their talent, still had to put in decades of work before they were able to build a strong foundation of success. It's time to check our entitlement at the door. Real winners aren't built overnight. First place is a title that must be hard fought and hard won.

Stress not only helps us get to the winner's circle, but it also gives us the strength to stay there. In fact, a group of scientists undertook a study about Earth's living systems using a biosphere, which allowed them to witness the growing patterns of trees. One of the most profound things they discovered had to do with the wind's role in a tree's life. Pay attention to what happened when trees grew up in the biosphere, shielded from the pain of the natural elements:

> The trees inside Biosphere 2 grew rapidly, more rapidly than they did outside of the dome, but they also fell over before reaching maturation. After looking at the root systems and outer layers of bark, the scientists came to realize that a lack of wind in Biosphere 2 caused a deficiency of stress

wood. Stress wood helps a tree position itself for optimal sun absorption and it also helps trees grow more solidly. Without stress wood, a tree can grow quickly, but it cannot support itself fully. It cannot withstand normal wear and tear, and survive. In other words, the trees needed some stress in order to thrive in the long run.[2]

Isn't that fascinating? So what are we doing for kids when we shield them from pain, loss, or failure? We think we're protecting them, but what if we are actually weakening them and stunting their growth?

So what if you won your fourth-grade spelling bee? Or if you were voted most valuable player on your high school soccer team? What are you doing to build yourself into a winner right now? The greatest indicator of success is longevity, and longevity is only achieved by taking small, meaningful, consistent steps in the same direction.

If you have yet to see the kind of achievements you're looking for in your life, ask yourself if you have put in the time. Get really honest with yourself about this. You can't expect the instant gratification of social media. You may never be "liked" or starred or applauded for the work you put in this morning. But one day, when you stand in front of your peers and heroes, holding that trophy, no one will be able to deny that you've done it.

You can't fake the work. You will know—and so will everyone else—that you deserve to be standing there. You are a champion.

Success Leads to Success

One of the great things about success is that each little success leads to the next success and then the next one and the next one. It's like building blocks. You need dozens to build something meaningful. One door opens another door, which opens another.

Take Richard Branson, for example. Branson's first business venture was a simple magazine called *Student*, which he founded at age sixteen. He later set up a mail-order record business, which led to a chain of record stores a few years after that. (You might have heard of Virgin Records.) The Virgin brand eventually grew to include an airline, a music label, and even a health-care company.

Do you think Branson knew as a young high school student starting *Student* magazine that he would eventually be knighted? I doubt it. Do you think he ever imagined he would have an airline? A record label? A health-care company? Do you think he could have predicted that he would be listed as one of Great Britain's Greatest Britons (according to a 2002 BBC poll)? I doubt it. He just reached for what was in front of him. That success led to another success, which led to another success, which led to another.

Michael Bloomberg is another man who took this strategy of using one success to build toward something. You might know Bloomberg as the 108th mayor of New York, but you might not realize how he got there. Bloomberg went to Johns Hopkins University, where he graduated with honors, and then went to Harvard Business School. In 1973, he became a partner in the securities brokerage Salomon Brothers, where he headed investment banking and then systems development.

But in 1981, Salomon Brothers was bought by Phibro, and Bloomberg was laid off without any severance. Using the equity money from being a partner in the firm, Bloomberg set up a company named Innovative Market Systems, and Merrill Lynch became its first customer in 1982. Lots of hard work and slow growth later, the company has over three hundred twenty-five thousand terminal subscribers worldwide.

Bloomberg is now worth $47.5 billion and is one of the top ten richest men in the United States.

When you break this down, you realize that most of the people who have been really successful didn't come with platinum spoons in their mouths.

Success comes from simply reaching for the next thing, trusting one little success will lead to another one and to another.

The Long Road

You do not have to be the greatest to finish first. You only have to be the best you've ever been. You have to be better than you were yesterday.

So often when we look at success, we see the incredible virtuoso musicians or athletes. What we don't see is the long road they walked to get there. We don't see the time they put in while we weren't watching. We see Michael Jordan in a Nike commercial, but we don't see the more than nine thousand shots he missed to get to the game-winning shot we all remember.

To run a marathon, you'll have to take 55,334 steps before you get to the finish line. Not to mention all the steps you take in the training process before the actual race! You didn't see me show up for 31,200 practices—just as an amateur, before I even turned pro. Of those practice sessions, one-third were free-skating sessions where I would fall an average of four times per session. That means I fell 41,600 times. And then I got back up and kept skating.

Winning starts at the starting line—not at the finish line. We can get so focused on the finish line that we forget everything that comes before it. We can get so caught up with our failures that we don't even give ourselves permission to keep putting one foot in front of the other. There are a thousand finish lines along the way, not just one. Each day is a finish line. Each practice is a finish line. Each little decision is a finish line.

I dare you to take that first step toward your own version of success. I can't guarantee what will happen next, but I can promise you won't regret it. This is where grace lives—in the jumping in. In showing up, day after day. In trying and learning and trying again and again.

CHAPTER 5

KEEP SHOWING UP

For me, winning isn't something that happens
suddenly on the field when the whistle blows
and the crowds roar. Winning is something that
builds physically and mentally every day that
you train and every night that you dream.

–EMMITT SMITH[1]

It's tempting at times to look around and think that everyone is getting where they're going faster than you are, that they're finding more success than you, and that you must be doing something wrong. What if it's just taking longer for you to get to the finish line than you first expected?

What if winning was so much less about having the right qualities and qualifications and more about simply having the hunger to win? What if it was less about hard work and sacrifice and more about commitment and repetition? Would the concept of winning become easier for you if you believed it was simply about getting on the right path and doing the same things over and over again?

Will you stay the course?

On the path to success, things won't always go exactly as you plan. It doesn't happen at ludicrous speed. But when we put our lives in God's hands—when we give ourselves to His purpose—He promises to make it all matter for something.

In 1976, I decided I wanted to get ahead of my competitors by doing a jump no one was doing at that time: the triple Lutz. In practice, I fell on my right hip so many times attempting the jump that I developed a cyst on my right side. The swelling went from just above the outside of my right knee to all the way above my hip. Eventually I was forced to have surgery, which was not only painful but also set me back months in my training. Not to mention it set me up for a devastating loss in 1977—a year when I was expected, and expecting, to win.

I had put everything on that one jump. It became an idol. The problem was, when I began to see the jump slipping from my grasp, as well as my expectations for 1977, I lost motivation and went back to my old ways of underperforming. I was partying with my friends and having fun rather than taking my training seriously.

Not surprisingly, I lost that year at Nationals. It was my fault. I knew it was. Then, after that loss, things got even worse than I expected they could. Tragedy struck in my life.

In May 1977, I lost my mom to cancer. And losing her changed everything for me.

Pain is motiving. Loss is motivating. The life you don't want becomes a firm foundation for the life you do want.

In 1978, I finally mastered the triple Lutz—mostly because even after the surgery on my injured hip, it hurt too much to fall. I showed up that year ready for battle. I took my mom with me to every practice in spirit. She held me accountable. And when I showed up to competition in 1978, I became the first person in the world to land a triple Lutz in the short program.

At Sectionals that year, the top three men were forced to compete instead of going straight to the National Championships. I was the first one to skate the short program. My sponsor, Frank McLoraine, told me two things: One, the first shall be last and the last shall be first (I didn't understand that at all at the time). And, two, to take what the ice gave me. I relaxed going into that first triple Lutz and won the short program over the top three guys in the country.

I went from ninth place in the United States in 1977 to third place in the United States in 1978—and achieved eleventh place at the World Championships that same year.

The circumstances you face in your life and in your work that are not ideal become the very reason you decide to be a champion. This is how it was for me. Even in the face of overwhelming loss, I kept showing up, doing the work, being the kind of man I knew I wanted to be. The rest took care of itself.

The Roller Coaster

In 1979, right after the World Championships, my coach decided to take on my biggest competitor—one of the guys I would need to beat to make it to World Championships the next year and the Olympic team in 1980. That meant that now I would be skating with him, on the same ice, every day at practice. Which meant practice wouldn't be practice anymore. It would be competition—*every day.*

I started to do what anybody would do if they were competing against their biggest competitor every day. I began overworking myself. Practicing too hard. Pushing myself too far. It was a setup for an injury.

When attempting to do a jump my competitor had done that I hadn't, I landed forward, still rotating, and tore every single ligament in my right ankle, which put me behind physically and politically. Again. Notice how many ups and downs can occur when you are on your path to finishing first. People often complain to me that they must not be "made" to win because they keep experiencing so many setbacks. Constant setbacks are *part* of this process. An expected part. A necessary part.

Of course, with the injury, that season didn't go as planned. And after a disappointing fourth place at Nationals, my coach lost interest in me. I could feel it happening, even if he wouldn't say it. Things were about to get worse for me before they could get better.

Repeat, Repeat, Repeat

After my fourth-place finish at the 1979 Nationals, I knew I needed to speak with my coach. I was grateful that he saved my skating life and showed initial interest, but things had changed. I told him that my sponsors had informed me they would support me if I left to take lessons from Mr. Laws in Philadelphia. I asked my coach straight out if he was still interested in teaching me. What came next let me know exactly where he stood in our coach–student relationship. He said that Mr. Laws was his friend, and if I wanted to take lessons from him, he wouldn't be upset or try to hurt me politically. What he never said was "stay." I was obviously expendable. The rejection was equally painful as it was liberating.

This was disturbing for me, yet I couldn't blame him. I felt as though I had let him down.

I wondered how I was ever going to become great at anything given the fact that this was the best opportunity I'd ever been given, and I had blown it. Again.

There are moments in life when you arrive at a crossroads. Either you can keep doing the same thing you've been doing and get the same results, or you can make a change and watch your life change. Once again, I decided I was going to do the second. Notice how many times I had to make the same decision over and over again, how many times I had to fall and get up again. This is a key element in finishing first. Each time you make the choice to win, the decision sinks deeper.

I found another coach—a man who didn't have the pedigree of a world championship coach necessarily, but he was president of the International Professional Skaters Union and was also a friend and willing to help. Once again I made a decision, right then and there, that I was done underachieving. I was ready for change. I was ready to accept this new opportunity. I was done being the person who would go only halfway or commit to something but not follow through. I was going to continue to honor every sacrifice my mom had made for me, everything she had invested in me. Once again I was going to prove her right—she was the one who had spent her whole life loving me so I would be the best I could be.

Don Laws was my new coach, and most of what he taught me didn't have to do with skating but with what it took to be a winner. I desperately needed that from him. As before, I needed someone to be hard on me, to give me some structure, and to expect more from me than anyone had ever expected. He taught me how to be on time, to take myself seriously, to use every minute on the ice because ice time is gold. Actually, he would say it's beyond gold. It's platinum. Don't waste it, he would urge me.

He is the one who taught me that to be the skater I wanted to be, I had to be the person I wanted to be. He saw something in me I couldn't see in myself—the same way my mom had. And this, as it turns out, was exactly what I needed. But I had to agree. Again and again, day in and day out, I had to make the same decisions and keep showing up.

That year, at my first international competition of the

year, my expectations for myself were pretty conservative. I thought, if I came in fifth, that would be good. But when it came time to skate, I surprised myself. I'd never done a clean program like that before. I actually beat the guy who ended up winning the silver medal that year at the Olympics. I won!

For me, that was all it took—a taste. Now I could see my path. So I started focusing on what I needed to do to get over the next obstacle in front of me. I started becoming a champion.

Protect Your Goal

What does showing up and doing the work look like for you today? Would it mean making that call you've been putting off? Sending those e-mails you've been avoiding? Going to the gym for the first time in a week?

When someone wants to go to a movie at 10:00 p.m. but you have practice at 6:00 the next morning, what is your response? Are you going to squeeze it in, losing sleep to make it all work? Or are you committed to being fully present at practice the next day? You can have whatever you want, but you can't have everything. You have to make a choice about what's important to you.

Let me tell you what sets a true champion apart from a wannabe: What happens when it's time to show up to do the work? Are you there—in mind, body, and spirit—or are you somewhere else? When your friends call to see if you want to take a long lunch on a workday, what choice do you make? If you're satisfied with how things are, you'll say yes. You'll rearrange your work time so that you can fit them in. If you're a champion, the answer is, "I'm busy." It's not that you can have no friends or no life, it's just, "I'm busy during work time. Work time is work time."

Once I got into the rhythm of being accountable to something bigger than myself, showing up for practice wasn't a question. I wasn't just showing up most of the time anymore. I was showing up all the time. And I wasn't just showing up mostly. I was showing up completely—mind, body, and spirit. I started getting more out of my practice time and began to see my progress double and triple. I was getting better, faster.

Any of us can make excuses about why we can't or aren't showing up in a real way to our priorities, but at the end of the day, there is no denying who was there and who wasn't. You can't fake this. You either did the work or you didn't. You were either present or you weren't. And when it comes time to compete, it's clear who has put in the time and who has half-heartedly hoped that their meager efforts will be rewarded with an undeserved victory.

Mike Dee is an old friend who I used to hang out with while I lived in Philadelphia, training for the 1980 Olympics. He was a former skater who was going to college for business. When I would ask him to go to a movie with me, he would say, "I can't. I'm studying for a competition." Meaning he had a test coming up.

He had a work ethic that remains to this day. He was

willing to sacrifice and put in the time. Today he is one of the most successful people I know in business, and he climbs mountains and rides bikes and is a top performer in everything he does. He's an inspiration to me and so many others.

I heard of a young man who moved to Nashville because he needed a big change in his life. He's recovering from an addiction to prescription drugs and wants to be a musician. Nashville, of course, is the most competitive market for musicians, but he moved there anyway, trusting that with commitment and repetition he could make progress toward his goal.

He's a drummer but took a job at a bank during the day to pay his bills. He found a cheap place to live and rented a storage unit where he keeps his drum set. Five days a week, after work, he leaves his job and drives to the storage unit, where he practices the drums for three hours at a time.

Coworkers ask him to hang out after work, and he says no. He is scheduled to go practice the drums. Friends ask him to dinner, and he says, "Sure, on the weekends. During the week, I work and play the drums." There is no confusion about priorities. No question about what is going to happen each week. No question in this young man's mind what his priorities are. That is commitment and repetition. And, as a result, I guarantee you that he will make a way for himself, even in Nashville's incredibly competitive music industry.

You might be thinking, *Okay, I want to be a winner, but I also want to have a life.* My question for you is this: Do you want the same life you've been living, or do you want a different one? The fact that you're this far into the book tells me that you want a different one. You're not satisfied.

You're ready for a change. That's what we're talking about here. We're talking about making a change—small changes, really—so you can have the life you've always wanted.

You might also be wondering, *But what about my friends?* Let me be blunt with you for a minute. If your friends are constantly trying to pull you off your path, there's a very good chance that those friends are losers and want you to be too. The life of a champion is not a life without friendship, but it is a life that requires you to decide who your friends are going to be. You're not going to choose people who distract you from finishing first with pointless pursuits, such as bar hopping and hanging out until all hours of the night. No true champion has the time or energy for that. You're too busy, too focused.

I've read countless accounts of people who have arrived on the shores of this country, not able to speak one word of English, who have become magnificent entrepreneurs. So much of it, I think, is that they know that if they don't, they're not going to eat. Necessity is an incredible motivator.

Too many of us lack drive not because we don't have what it takes but because we're too comfortable. We think, *I'm not going to get anything more for working hard, so what's the point?* The point is that you've got one life to live. This is not a dress rehearsal. It's your only shot. There's a beginning, a middle, and an end. And our job is to make the middle as great as possible.

There Are No Rainmakers

Sometimes I come across people who think that because a person has experienced success, he or she is some sort of rainmaker. They think the person has the Midas touch and that everything this individual puts his or her hands on turns to gold.

Or they attribute the person's success, at least partially, to "luck." How lucky that person was, we tell ourselves, to be in the right place at the right time, or to have shaken hands with that right person, or to have gained momentum or attention for what they are working on.

This translates, at times, to people wanting to jump on whatever bandwagon they think will advance their cause. They want to ride coattails to victory. Many of these people even have pure motives and generous goals. They're raising money for cancer research, for example, or wanting to get a positive message out to the world.

But I have to break the disappointing news to you that there is nothing magic about success. It won't do you any good to hitch your wagon to someone else's star. There is only one explanation for a meaningful body of work: commitment to the process.

The successful people put in the time. They are willing to do the work. Luck is fine. But luck is not a strategy. To be in the right place at the right time, you have to be in the right place all of the time. Over and over again.

Each day is a collection of minutes. Each year is a collection of days.

These are all bricks in the wall you're building. What are your bricks made of?

No matter what you're trying to do, you're not going to be able to see results overnight. The question is, Are you willing to do the things other people aren't willing to do? Are you willing to put in the time? Are you willing to do the work? The reason I've raised so much money for cancer is because I've spent sixteen years banging on doors, asking the hard questions, asking for favors, hitting the streets. People think this success is magic. It's not magic. It's simply a commitment to the process.

During my first years of being a professional skater, one year I was on the road for twelve months. The next year I was on the road for eleven months. Which means that between those two years, I had one month off the road. I kept showing up, working hard, doing what I knew it took to be successful. So little of that was big and flashy. I just knew I had a job to do, and I did it.

The bad news about this is that there is no magic pill or concept that offers you a sure-fire breakthrough. The good news is you don't need any of those things. You may have heard the quote from Thomas Edison that says, "Opportunity is missed by most people because it is dressed in overalls and looks like work." Success is not rocket science. Anyone can do it. Anyone, that is, who is willing to do the work.

While crowd-watching on my family's trip to Disney World, I caught myself thinking about how that amazing park wouldn't have been there without the strong and faithful vision of Walt Disney. It all started with one man. He just drew a cartoon. He worked hard, put in the time, and kept showing up again and again. And look at what he has to show for it today. His legacy lasts even beyond him. His joy is spreading in a contagious way, even after he's left this world.

When you decide to become a winner, you forfeit the right to complain. Do it for the love of the game, or the art, or the business. Or don't do it at all. You can keep losing if you want to. You can have your ten minutes in the spotlight. I know that so many of you reading this, like me, want more. You don't want to have a short shelf life. You want longevity. You want to truly make a difference.

Once I started working with Don Laws, I started to work like a champion. I felt a tremendous amount of guilt for having been such a lousy competitor while my mom was alive, and I began to see how all of my self-sabotaging, lazy, and entitled ways weren't just sad, but they were actually wrong. Suddenly I felt myself growing up physically, mentally, emotionally, and spiritually. Almost overnight, I developed a maturity—like a boy turning into a man.

People often say things to me like, "I don't have the discipline to be a champion," "I'm a procrastinator," or "I'm just lazy." My response to them is the same. You're not lazy. You just haven't shown up yet. You haven't tapped that innate human drive for survival. That superhuman desire to see results. What would help you to access that part of yourself?

For some of us, that comes through tragedy. Losing my mom motivated me to action in a way nothing could before.

For some people, it's a life-threatening diagnosis that breaks them free from the mentality that they can't succeed. Others just wake up one day and decide they're tired of underselling themselves, tired of underperforming, tired of acting like they don't have what it takes. When we go from being terrified of failure to being terrified of never trying, we take the first steps to changing our lives forever.

Put in the Time

One of my biggest pet peeves when I did television commentary was when I heard coaches give their skaters instructions right before they headed onto the ice to compete. I often stood back and watched this happen and thought to myself, *It's too late. You're too late.* You can see it in the skater's eyes. The information is going in one ear and out the other. Or, even worse, it is scaring the skater into doing exactly what the coach is advising against. The coach is saying, "When you get to that jump, make sure to breathe—and don't drop your left shoulder." I can tell you exactly what's going to happen when the skater gets to the jump. He or she is going to drop the left shoulder.

By the time you've made it to the competition, it's too late to be making changes. You need time for the practice hours you've put in, the corrections, and the messages from your coaches to become a part of who you are, not just what you do. You need time for it all to sink in at the cellular level. There is no faking the process, no such thing as a shortcut. Any instruction from a coach or anybody else coming to you at the last minute is coming to you too late. If you have to think too hard about it, you've already lost.

I play golf with a friend in town, and he sometimes gets very critical of his golf game. When we were playing one day, he hit a drive that pulled to the left, and he let out the most frustrated sigh. "I can't believe I missed that shot!" he said. But I just looked at him.

"How many balls have we hit today?" I asked him. He looked a little confused but turned to me.

"Probably twenty or thirty."

"Yeah, if we hit one hundred balls today, and one hundred balls every day, then you could be mad at yourself for missing that shot. Otherwise, you're not allowed to be critical about this. The pros expect to hit a shot like that because they're hitting four hundred to five hundred balls per day. We're hitting twenty to thirty. You can't expect to be better than the time you put in."

The point is, if you don't put in the time it takes to be a champion, you can't be surprised when your performance doesn't reach champion heights. It takes tons of time and tons of practice, and there is no shortcutting or short-circuiting the process. If you want to be really good at something, you have to be consistent.

To practice your golf shot one hundred times is helpful. To practice it one thousand times is game changing. If real estate is about "location, location, location," then victory is about "repetition, repetition, repetition." When I decided to become a professional skater, it took me two years of endless experimentation to get to the place where I was no longer an amateur. That's how long it took for all the training to become a part of me, to get into my DNA. You can't fake that. There are no shortcuts.

You've either put in the time or you haven't.

There's a great metaphor by the author Simon Sinek, who became famous for his TED Talk "Start with Why" and his book with the same title. He talks about how the millennial generation has a way of seeing the summit of a mountain but not the mountain itself. This is the disease that keeps us from success. We see where we're trying to go, but we don't see what it actually takes to get there. We don't see the thousands of hours of training, we don't see the hundreds of thousands of steps to the top, and we don't see the time all of this takes before we actually reach the thing we are dreaming about.

If you are waiting until the last minute, procrastinating, and believe you can "cram" for a test, you are sabotaging your own success. If you haven't put in the time, you won't be able to perform. A brick wall can't be built with a single brick (unless you're an ant)—and your dream won't be accomplished with a single step. It's all the tiny little steps that add up over time.

This is the mind-set that starts opening doors for you. One open door leads to another, which leads to another. They build on each other. To think you're going to build a whole career on a single success is like thinking you're going to build a brick wall with one brick.

In September 1979, I began to see all of my consistency and dedication begin to pay off. I had been working to become a better skater for long enough at that point to finally begin to see results. By the time Nationals came around in January 1980, I found my way to the podium, placing third. This was not only the best I had ever done, but it was also good enough to put me on the Olympic team. In February, I competed at the Olympics and took fifth. Now I was starting to be the kind of skater other skaters were watching.

Too many people are looking for growth to be explosive, when the truth is that real growth happens slowly. If you think growth happens overnight, you'll get frustrated when you don't see immediate results, and you will give up. When you recognize that growth happens over time, you make the choice to show up, act like a champion, and live like a champion every day. There are no shortcuts on the path to success. There is no faking it. You've either done the work or you haven't.

When you step out on the ice, it's just you. Most of us are used to being managed, coached, held up by friends or family members, or reinforced by titles or positions. But when it comes time to compete, you're the only one out there. There's nothing to hide behind. How you show up to practice will be how you show up to a competition. How you choose to live your life will be how you show up on the day you're called to perform.

And if you put in the work off the field, or outside of the office, there will be no question that you are a champion. You may not win everything all at once. But you will make slow, steady progress in the right direction. Eventually you will get there. And it won't have been handed to you. You will have earned it.

CHAPTER 6

OVERCOME YOUR LIMITATIONS

*I cannot discover that anyone knows enough
to say definitely what is and is not possible.*

—HENRY FORD[1]

In 1984, I was invited to speak at the Paralympic Games celebration dinner in Denver, Colorado. It was just after I had come home from my Olympic gold win in Sarajevo, and I showed up with my chest held high, basking in all of my Olympic fabulousness, only to be greeted by a room full of athletes who, without saying anything, made me realize how much I still had to learn about being a champion.

As the dinner unfolded, the feeling that I was "amazing" quickly faded. I looked around the room at a group of people who had overcome the most impossible obstacles, obstacles I couldn't even imagine, to stand in the winner's circle. I was reminded within a minute of what it really means to be a champion.

Paralympic athletes do things most people could never imagine.

They go down mountains on one leg at seventy miles per hour. They play hockey in sleds, sitting on a skate, without the ability to use their legs. They play basketball in wheelchairs. These athletes have pretty much any physical disability you can imagine, and yet they compete at an extremely high level— beyond anything most of us would dare dream. Winning is about tapping into your innate human potential.

This is a lesson to all of us that it is not a lack of skill or talent or capability or know-how that keeps us from achieving our own personal victory. It's a lack of bravery, a lack of willing- ness to put all of our cards on the table. If we could only get over our excuses, we would find that we have always been the champions we long to be. We've been holding back.

What if you were able to achieve the kind of personal potential in your life that Paralympic athletes achieve in their lives every day? We can rise above not only expectation but also the things that normally would hold anyone back. Winning is not normal. But it's so important.

A champion says, "I will not let my limitations keep me from achieving my dreams. I will make the impossible possible." This is what the athletes of the Paralympic Games are doing every day. Why is it taking so long for us to get it?

The Only Disability

The only disability in life is a bad attitude. I repeat this over and over again to the skaters I work with, to my kids, and to anyone who will listen, really. That's how important I think it is. This approach to life can be the difference between winning and losing, between first place and last place.

No matter who you are and no matter what finishing first looks like for you, any goal will always have obstacles, difficulties, and setbacks. You will be defined not by those setbacks but by how you respond to them.

You can decide ahead of time—before you even set out on your journey—that this is going to be "too hard," and you will be right. Or you can learn to identify setbacks as minor problems that you need to put behind you and decide to have a good time doing whatever it is you are doing. I mean, if you're not having fun doing something, then why are you doing it? If succeeding means it's going to be a horrible, awful, painful ordeal for you, then why would you do it? I don't believe success is gained this way.

You'll meet some people in life who seem to have a miserable time no matter what they're doing. They could be on a vacation at the beach, and they would still find something to complain about. The towels at the resort weren't big enough. The hotel staff weren't friendly enough. The weather was too hot or too cold. Then you'll meet other people who tackle life's biggest obstacles with incredible tenacity—and smile and laugh their way through it. It's not a difference in circumstance; it's a difference in perspective. Attitude is everything.

Of course there will be hard moments on the way. Of course there will be moments when you have to do things you don't want to do. But you can choose either to see these moments as small blips on the radar of the overall adventure of your life or to focus on them, blow them out of proportion, and make them the entire scope of the landscape. The best thing a champion can do is maximize the good moments and minimize the uncomfortable ones. This is the fastest, best, most fun way to the top.

Who Says It's Impossible?

I recently learned about a young man named Kyle Maynard who wanted to climb to the top of Mount Kilimanjaro. The feat itself is impressive but not impossible. It would take some training, strengthening, and preparation. Thousands of other people have climbed to the top. He had amazing role models to follow. There was only one difference. Kyle was born with no arms or legs.

For Kyle, the climb to the top of Mount Kilimanjaro would be far greater than just training and preparation. It would be a nearly impossible feat, one that had never been attempted before. The question on everyone's mind as Kyle began to push toward his goal was, Will he be able to overcome his obvious limitations to achieve his dream?

Maybe you can relate in some way to Kyle's dilemma. There's something you want to achieve. Maybe it's something hundreds or thousands of other people have done before you. But the lingering "problem" in the back of your mind is that you have an obvious limitation you can't ignore. Maybe you don't have the money or the reputation or the experience or the resources to do the thing you want to do.

As a cancer survivor, any time I meet people who have been diagnosed with cancer, I assure them that there will be a moment in the beginning when they feel gripped with fear. Then, suddenly, without explanation, that fear will morph into an inexplicable drive to survive. I tell them that before they know it, they will find more strength, more resilience, and more fight inside of them than they ever dreamed possible. We are capable of so much more than we realize.

You don't have to be diagnosed with a life-threatening illness to uncover your own inner resilience. All you need is to know what you truly desire, what you want badly enough that you're willing to do anything to get it. Then you begin to deal with the obstacles and "limitations" getting in your way—and decide that you're finished with letting anything keep you from living the life you want to live.

Nothing but Solutions

In 2014, when the Nashville Predators decided to get into a new venture of managing ice-skating centers, they asked me if I would be willing to partner with them in building a "Learn to Skate" program. I, of course, agreed. In the process of building the Scott Hamilton Skating Academy, Paula Trujillo, who was the facilitator and who handled all the details, experienced firsthand the worst of the obstacles and setbacks. Imagine trying to facilitate the schedules of dozens of different coaches and students, making sure there are no overlaps, and that everyone gets what they need. It couldn't have been easy.

Still, Paula would always say, "There are no problems. There are only solutions." Isn't that true? Problems are only a test for how creative we can get with our solutions.

How creative can you get with the solutions to your problems?

The most successful people do not necessarily have the most resources or the most talent. They're the ones who have leveraged hidden strategies perfect for their individual skill sets.

Nathan Chen is the "it" guy in skating right now—a seventeen-year-old US champion who has more jumps than anybody in the world. That's the "it" factor for this kid. His jumps. He can just keep putting most of his eggs in that basket. If he keeps doing jumps, and doing them better than anyone else, that's his "ace" card to win.

I recently met George Shinn, who is also a cancer survivor. Given his background, he's the last person you would predict to finish first. But the man has amazing tenacity. He was born in North Carolina to a poor family and graduated last in his class of 293 students from A. L. Brown High School.

He worked in a textile mill and as a school janitor to pay his way through Evans Business College. Then—get this—upon graduating from Evans, he bought the school.

Purchased it, along with several other small colleges, which he consolidated under the company name Rutledge Education Systems.

Eventually he ended up selling the school and buying a basketball team with the proceeds. If you recognize his name, it's probably because he later became the owner of the Charlotte Hornets. Then, in 1973, he founded the George Shinn Foundation, whose mission and purpose is to provide scholarships for the under-resourced.

Look around. Pay attention to the stories of people who are finishing first. Then realize that all of your excuses are just that—excuses. Ask what has worked for others and how you can make it work for you, too. Ask yourself how you can leverage your unique skills and strengths to accomplish the unthinkable. How can you go from the bottom of your class to purchasing the school?

Kenny Troutt is the founder of Excel Communications and a billionaire who started with nothing. His dad was a bartender, and he paid his way through college by selling life insurance. He was willing to get over his "ego" and do whatever was necessary to get from point A to point B.

Howard Schultz, the chief executive officer of Starbucks, grew up in a housing complex for the poor and started his business career selling copiers for Xerox. Even at Xerox, Schultz quickly became one of the top sellers and was promoted to full sales representative. He had the charisma and the charm to win people over and get them to buy anything. Even a copy machine.

Oprah Winfrey was born into poverty to an unmarried teenage mother and raised for her first six years by her maternal grandmother, who it is said was so poor that Oprah sometimes wore potato sacks as dresses. At thirteen, after years of suffering from abuse, Oprah ran away from home. In the face of persecution and bullying at school, Oprah was unwilling to give up. She eventually landed a job in radio and later became the first African American television correspondent in Nashville, Tennessee. Then, in 1993, she was recruited to work for an AM radio talk show that would eventually become known as the *Oprah Winfrey Show.*

Ralph Lauren started as a clerk at Brooks Brothers, only dreaming of men's ties. What a great reminder that it always starts with a dream. If you feel like you're being called to something, answer it. A dream you don't answer becomes a nightmare.

People look at success stories of those who came from nothing and become something great and think about how they must have been really special. Why can't this be you?

Slay Your Dragons

Whatever you think is holding you back is not holding you back. You can use it to your advantage. Abuse. Bullying.

Poverty. Lack of education. Bad grades. Anything. It can't be a bigger obstacle than what Oprah was facing, or Schultz, or Kenny Troutt. When you start to pay attention, you find story after story of people who had to wait their turn. They simply stayed in the game long enough to win.

The tennis player Jimmy Connors was famous for saying, "All I need is one break—once I get one service break, I win." That was his mentality. What if this was your mentality? The only other choice you really have is to quit. How often has quitting worked as a strategy?

Of course you are going to encounter obstacles—forks in the road, moments when you have to make a decision whether to move right or left. Critics and failure and all kinds of weights will try to pull you down and hold you back. You will develop the strength you need to slay these dragons.

The thing with fire is that you can either be consumed by it or be the rocket fueled by it. The same water that softens a potato hardens an egg. Same substance. Different results. And it all has to do with who you decide to be. There's not a person out there who doesn't have a mountain of pain he or she is dealing with. There's not a person who doesn't have critics. It's how you deal with it. Are you going to let it hold you back? Or are you going to use it to propel you toward your great purpose in this life?

What is holding you back? Are you late to your commitments? Are you easily distracted? Do you need to work on communication skills? Do you make impulsive decisions? Even something as simple as the way you present yourself to people can have a huge impact on your ability to finish first. Rather than overlook your weaknesses, become someone who is worthy of winning by overcoming them.

When it came to climbing Mount Kilimanjaro, Kyle Maynard's attitude was, "Every excuse we make keeps us from getting what we want most out of life."[2]

How many people have this attitude about overcoming challenges? It is this attitude that drove all of Kyle's training and sent him to Tanzania, where he would attempt something that, for most people, would have seemed impossible. Maybe even crazy.

Possibly the greatest day of your adult life is when you walk into a living space that *you* are paying for. Not your parents. Not anyone else. You. There's no feeling like it. Even if life will give you handouts, you'll never be satisfied with getting things for which you didn't have to work to have them. You are craving a challenge, aren't you?

I believe we all are wired for struggle. And until you make the decision to fight for what really matters to you, you're going to continue wondering if you're missing something. You were made to answer the bell.

If you're totally satisfied with your life, if you don't feel you need to make any changes, then do me a favor and hand this book off to someone who can really benefit from it. But if you look at where you are and it's not exactly where you want to be, then ask yourself what it would look like for you to show up—in mind, body, and spirit—to what you are wanting to do.

All you have to do is look around. Examples of people who

show up every day are everywhere. Every athlete you admire, every businessperson you admire, every leader you admire shows up in ways you probably don't even know. Because it's not dramatic. There's not a bunch of fanfare. Nobody gives you an award or a trophy for doing the work. It's just commitment and repetition, a dedication to showing up and doing the same things, day after day.

Kyle Maynard didn't climb Kilimanjaro by deciding he was at the summit. It was one day at a time, one step at a time. It was with an iron will that Kyle climbed (or more like bear-crawled) step after step up the 19,000-foot mountain. Consistency and repetition. He kept moving, unwilling to let anything throw him off course.

In January 2012, he completed his mission to climb the epic peak of Mount Kilimanjaro. Not only that, but he also carried with him the ashes of a fallen soldier who wanted to be sprinkled at the top. In that emotional moment at the top of the mountain, Kyle showed himself what is possible with simple commitment and repetition. He showed all of us. This is what happens when one person decides he has what it takes. Everyone leans in to share in the victory with him.

Are you ready to be done underachieving? Then it's time to choose to do something different. It's time to start showing up. It's time to be done waiting for the life you want to be handed and to start fighting for it. It's time to start believing that your limitations are just excuses.

You are capable. I know you are. It's time to start acting like it.

CHAPTER 7

OUTWORK EVERYONE

The key is not the will to win. Everybody has that.
It is the will to prepare to win that is important.

—BOBBY KNIGHT[1]

One of my greatest competitors in skating also happened to be one of the most naturally talented skaters the world has ever known. He had more natural ability than just about anyone else in the sport. He was literally built to skate. But he had one thing working against him: he loved smoking pot.

The morning I learned this was one of the greatest mornings of my life. I knew that I could never out-talent this guy, but because of his failure to address his weakness, I could outwork him. He didn't have the work ethic to make an easy choice. If you have the hunger to win, this isn't even a question. Your mind is made up.

I have known dozens of athletes in my career who had more talent and natural ability than I did. How was I able to beat them? I can only think that I wanted it more than they did. I learned how to outlast them when it came to commitment and dedication.

People often talk about the sacrifice it takes to win. I don't necessarily like to think of it like that because, in my mind, this is a no-brainer. Once your mind is made up that you want to finish first, the choices you have to make to get there are made for you. You stop making all the decisions that are sabotaging you.

Smoking pot isn't the only decision that will sabotage you. There are a thousand ways to sabotage your ability to be successful, and once you have made your mind up that you want to do it, you will. Anything that will keep you from your own ability to be successful is sabotage—procrastinating, drinking too much, not eating healthfully, showing up late, phoning it in, even just ignoring the instruction of your coach (or boss or teacher). This is all self-sabotage. When will you stop making decisions that are bad for you? When *you* decide you're ready to win.

Passing the Competition

You don't have to beat your competitors in every area in order to beat them. You just have to figure out what you have that they don't.

Leverage that.

What does Michael Jordan have that I don't? That's obvious. But what do I have that he doesn't? I'm short. It's a lot easier to steer a speed boat than an aircraft carrier. I will never be the basketball player Michael Jordan is, but if I want any chance of beating him, that's what I have to leverage—my strength, his weakness.

If you are running a business, look to your competition. What do they have that you don't have? Maybe your competitor has a formal education and you don't. But you have familiarity with your clientele and a track record. Maybe your competition has a lot of capital to invest, but you have time and a personal touch. Maybe what they have is a proven track record, but you have a hunger to succeed.

If a guy who graduates at the top of his class from Harvard wants to start a cancer foundation, he's going to be really good at the structure of it. He might have the right connections, the perfect business plan; he will probably be really organized with his financials. But then you have the guy who lost the most important person in his life due to cancer. You have the guy who knows intimately and personally the cost of being a cancer survivor.

Who is going to be more successful? It depends.

You can't possibly win a game without paying close attention to your competition. But don't think for a minute that the person "favored" to win will automatically win. What doesn't seem like a strength can be a strength if you know how to leverage it. What doesn't seem like a weakness in your competitor can become a weakness when you get good at playing the game. Join the ranks of the hundreds of inspiring champions throughout history who beat all the odds, who leveraged their unique strengths and simply worked harder than anyone else to finish first.

"No, You Can't"

Take a look around you at the people who are achieving miraculous things despite all the odds. If you don't have inspiring people around you, get some. These stories are everywhere when you start looking for them.

Melinda Doolittle is a great example of this. You may know her as an *American Idol* finalist and successful recording artist. But Melinda didn't start out in that place. In fact, when Melinda was young, she wanted nothing more than to be in her church choir. The only problem was that she couldn't sing. Really and truly—could not sing. She was tone deaf. Her choir director would play a note on the piano and ask Melinda to mimic it, but she couldn't do it. No matter how many times she tried, she kept falling short.

This devastated Melinda. Finally, the choir director agreed to let her stand up on the stage with all the other singers, as long as she would only lip sync. She could mouth the words but was instructed not to sing a single note.

Melinda agreed but didn't give up on her dream. She refused to allow her weakness to hold her back. She told her mom she wanted to sing in her school talent show, and her mom told her that if she wanted that, she was going to have to work hard—and she was going to have to pray. She was going to have to believe in something greater than herself that was pulling her through, something big enough to help her overcome her supposed weakness.

So Melinda began to pray for the ability to hear and replicate the notes. She prayed for the ability to sing, and kept practicing, and kept trying, despite the fact that her dream seemed crazy and out of her reach. When it came time to sing at the talent show, Melinda stepped onstage. She did exactly what she had been practicing. She doesn't remember singing that day, she told me. She only remembers finishing and the audience on its feet in applause. That was the first time she realized she had done it. She could sing. From that day forward, she never looked back.

Your Greatest Strength

I've taught my kids from the time they were very little that the greatest strength is a lack of weakness. To this day, if I ask any of them, "What's the greatest strength?" they repeat back, "A lack of weakness." It's funny because the things we think are our weaknesses are rarely our weaknesses. It's like Art Berg famously said, "Impossible just takes a little bit longer."

Think about it for a minute. What is weakness exactly? There are endless examples of people who don't see their weakness as weakness at all, including Kyle Maynard, who trained for months toward his dream of climbing to the top of Mount Kilimanjaro, even though no one else had ever attempted this climb with no arms and no legs. Kyle's motto was, "No arms, no legs, no excuses."

Even when people told him he was crazy, even when the feat seemed impossible, even when his weaknesses appeared to be too much, he kept training. What excuses are you making about your "weaknesses" that are keeping you from your potential?

For me, my weakness was always about compulsory figures.

Compulsory figures are the drill where you carve a figure-eight pattern on the ice over and over and over again with your skates. The idea is that if you're doing them right, you should be able to carve the same pattern again and again. It's easy to tell how accurate you've been because you leave a trail on the ice.

From even my early days of skating, I hated compulsory figures. I wasn't very good at them and I thought they were boring and frustrating, so I avoided them. It wasn't until after my mom died that I began to see how avoiding figures was holding me back in a big way.

I meet people all the time who say they want to quit smoking but complain it's too hard. They tell me that they "can't" and that they've "tried everything" and nothing has worked. When I ask them why they want to quit, they tell me it's because they think they should. They know it's the right choice for their health. Then I ask them, "But do you really want to?" Their response is, "Not really." Now the whole thing makes more sense. You can't do anything unless the desire is greater than the "should."

We all have weaknesses, but they're really more like distractions. Distractions are meant to be overcome. We're made of better stuff than our distractions; we're designed to conquer our weaknesses, and if you're not doing that, no wonder you're miserable.

Kyle Maynard could have seen his disability as a weakness. Melinda Doolittle could have seen her early failures as weakness. Instead, they both decided to leverage their disadvantages toward a greater purpose—inspiring people all over the world to achieve their amazing potential. With each excruciating step up the mountain, Kyle's dedication shouted to the world that there isn't anything that can keep you from your goals if you're willing to show up, outwork everyone, and learn to consider weaknesses as strengths. With each note Melinda sang that brought audiences to their feet, she proved what is said in Philippians 4:13: "I can do all things through Him who gives me strength."

What if the weaknesses you have presumed you have aren't actually weaknesses? For example, I was always shorter than my competitors—which I presumed was a drawback. I could see my height as a detriment, or I could look at the fact that I'm quicker and I recover faster. I could look at my height as a weakness, but instead I choose to look at it as a strength—because I can.

You can either listen to the part of you that says you can't do this or decide to tune that out and do it anyway. You can either let your weaknesses hold you back or you can become an inspiration to others, like Melinda Doolittle. Like Kyle Maynard.

Worthy of the Title

After the 1980 season, the three medalists at the Olympics and World Championships decided to retire from competitive skating. I remember that I got up to have breakfast one morning and did the math. With me being fifth at the World Championships and the top three retiring, I was now ranked second in the world. Now, that was one great cup of coffee!

I had only one guy left to beat if I wanted to be my sport's champion: the amazing David Santee. As far as raw ability, he had me beat. In fact, the same year I came in dead last at novice Nationals, he came in third in senior men. He was a thirteen-year-old phenom who made it to the championship men's podium that year. He was truly remarkable. And if I wanted to win, I had to find a way to catch him.

One thing I knew about my opponent was that he was a genius at compulsory figures. I mentioned earlier how I felt about those compulsories. But now I wasn't allowed to hate figures anymore. Not if I wanted to be worthy of winning. Because if I wanted to take my results to the next level, I had to get past my weaknesses. And if I didn't have the raw talent to do it, I was going to have to outwork everybody.

So I started strategically working with Mr. Laws. We would run figures over and over again. And when it comes to compulsory figures, you can't hide. You are drawing lines on the ice for everyone to see. You can tell very easily if you are on your inside or outside edge, if the circles are the same size, and if they are lined up on an axis. You can see how close your tracings are. I worked and worked and worked—and with each improvement, I craved more improvement. It was so satisfying.

I took the training one day at a time, getting just a little bit better each day. I would stay at the rink longer or show up earlier. I would repeat everything until I got it right. I lost sight of all my distractions. And as soon as I developed this muscle, I had the confidence I needed to face my opponent. Maybe he was more talented than I was. But I knew that if I lost, it wouldn't be because I hadn't tried hard enough. I had outworked everybody.

This changed who I was as a skater. Actually, it changed who I was as a person. I started skating better, with more confidence, and I started carrying myself differently. My greatest weakness wasn't my greatest weakness anymore. I may not have been the strongest competitor in the competition, but I was getting there. Even if I didn't win, I was becoming someone who was worthy of the title.

What would it take for you to become worthy of a title? Are you willing to outwork everybody?

As for me, the year I decided to overcome my weakness in compulsory figures was the same year I beat David Santee for the first time. I finished first; he finished second—both at the World Championships and US Nationals. Competing against each other at that level pushed us both beyond what we thought was possible. It was a healthy competition, and he was one of my favorite people to compete with. He made me better. And I think I made him better, too.

The next year, when I returned to defend the national and world titles, was the first year I realized that if I didn't win the title, one of these other guys was going to win it instead. It made the whole thing so human. I wasn't competing against everyone in the world. It was just these guys.

And I began to feel a healthy sense of ownership. A sense of personal responsibility for setting the standard for what it meant to hold the title. Instead of making me feel entitled, defending the title made me feel motivated to keep working harder than I had ever worked before.

There was no way I would be able step onto Olympic ice with my head held high as I fought to win the gold if I didn't act like the champion I knew I was. There was no way I would be allowed to continue inspiring others to be the best version of themselves if I let my guard down now. I was a different guy. I was a champion. I was a winner.

This is the power of finishing first. This is the power of showing up, leveraging your strengths and weaknesses, and outworking everyone. My world would never be the same.

CHAPTER 8

DITCH FEAR AND CELEBRATE FAILURE

Far better is it to dare mighty things, to win glorious triumphs,
even though checkered by failure, than to rank with those
poor spirits who neither enjoy nor suffer much, because they
live in the gray twilight that knows not victory nor defeat.

—THEODORE ROOSEVELT[1]

Looking back to the year I lost my mom, I was able to view life differently than when she was alive. I became a different skater because I became a different person. I think the biggest difference was that I wasn't scared anymore. The worst thing that could happen to me had already happened, and now I was playing with greater purpose. What will it take for you to decide that you're more afraid of staying stuck than you are of what it will take to become a winner?

Deep inside we know what winning requires of us. We

know that it's not a one-time event, but it's something we have to keep living up to over and over and over again. And rather than face the challenge of that, many of us sabotage our own success before we even get there.

There isn't a champion out there who doesn't struggle with the same insecurities you have. I'll never forget, after winning the World Championship, I felt that skating must be at its lowest point in history if I was the champion, and I needed to "up my game" now. My coach Don Laws recognized my insecurities immediately and knew this was going to be an even greater challenge to deal with than winning the World Championship. The way we see ourselves is often different than the way others see us. Don needed me to see that the World Championship was just another event. If I didn't win it, somebody else would.

Every champion wonders if he has what it takes. It's a very human thing. But this doesn't stop us from being hungry and aggressive—ready to do our work. That's what I want to help you understand. The process of becoming a champion is not rocket science. Champions are all people.

They're just people who have been willing to get past their fears and doubts because they're tired of being losers and are ready to win.

Yes, You Will Fall

The first thing we teach skaters when they come to the Scott Hamilton Skating Academy, no matter how old they are and no matter what their skill level, is how to fall and how to get up. Because you're going to fall. That is inevitable. And when you fall, the question is, how will you respond?

Finishing first is not the opposite of failure but rather the act of recovering from failures until those falls become your greatest strength. If you can do this, you have a superpower. No one will ever be able to beat you.

I've faced my fair share of failure. In fact, one of the things I've had to learn is that no amount of winning makes you immune to failure. The goal isn't to begin failing less but to learn how to be better at facing failure so we can leverage our failures as our best opportunities to learn. Even after I started to get some winning under my belt, I still had failure waiting for me around the corner.

When I travel and speak at events—often to rooms of highly successful businesspeople, chief executive officers, Olympic athletes, or influencers of some kind—I always ask the same question: "How many of you in this room have failed?" Inevitably, every single hand in the room shoots up.

The most successful people in the world know the most about failure because you will be hard-pressed to achieve any measure of success without also spending your fair share of time at the bottom of the barrel.

Ask Dave Ramsey, who turned his own financial ruin into a ministry helping people find their way out of debt. His listeners now amount to an estimated 12 million people weekly. Having spent time with him and his wife, Sharon, I know that they live as they instruct others to live and now he has a net worth I couldn't begin to estimate.

Why have we made a villain out of failure? Where along the way did we decide that failure was a bad thing? How can we not see how damaging this is to ourselves, to our culture, and to the generations coming after us? When we paint the picture that falling or missing the mark or losing the game is the worst thing that could happen, we miss everything failure has to offer us. Failure can become our greatest asset the minute we decide to wake up and not look at it as a villain.

You're not going to do anything right the first time. Or maybe you'll get lucky, and you will, but you'll be hard-pressed to replicate that the second time around. And the danger in this way of thinking is that you'll be so worried about failing that you won't try. Or you will try and will see your supposed failure as yet another reason why you weren't made to be a champion rather than see it for what it is: the best lesson anyone could ever give you on how to become better.

Failure Is a Requirement for Finishing First

Failure comes with the territory. Do you believe that? Not only should we expect lots and lots of failure, but we should also be grateful when it shows up because it means we are on the right track. Failure is a mile marker on the pathway to finishing first.

Look into the lives of the people you admire and respect, and you'll see more failure than you'd expect. You know Abraham Lincoln as one of the greatest presidents in American history. He led the country through great moral and military crises and played a critical role in the freedom of slaves. But did you know that Lincoln failed at business twice, lost when he ran for Congress, lost twice running for Senate, and suffered from what most would call a nervous breakdown?

You likely know Kurt Warner as the quarterback who led the St. Louis Rams to Super Bowl victory in 2000. But did you know that Kurt went undrafted in 1994 and took a job at a grocery store, where he made minimum wage? These are the stories you rarely hear about people who have achieved great success. The road to success is paved with a lot of failure.

Ulysses S. Grant is most well known for being elected twice to the presidency of the United States. What most people don't know about him is that he drank too much, battled with depression, and was an army dropout. After that, he suffered multiple business failures before being asked to return to the army for the Civil War, at which point he was quickly promoted to the top general of the Union forces before being elected to the presidency. If you start asking the people you admire most for the stories behind their successes, you'll find more failure than you ever dreamed possible.

This is why I teach the skaters who come to the Academy not to give failure too much attention. If they fall, I teach them not to make a big deal out of it. I tell them to get up and move on. Right away. Because the minute we start giving failure too much attention, we begin to move in its direction. Failed? No big deal. Let your failure fade into the background. Let's get up and try again.

Think about this. If a baseball player fails two-thirds of the time, he's in the hall of fame. And have you ever heard of a golfer shooting an 18? Not even the great golfers do this. No one expects them to. Why should we think it would be any different for us? Success is not meant to be an every-time thing. That's what makes it unique. The more times you try, the more likely you are to hit that one moment of success.

Nobody expects you to get it perfect every time. To become great at anything—a sport, an instrument, a job—you have to practice, do your drills, and keep showing up and trying again. You have to mess up and course correct, and, eventually, you do get it right. Your successes will be remembered far more than your failures. The failures eventually fade in their significance. But to get there, you have to keep going. You have to get up and try again.

Lose with Grace

One of my favorite all-time Olympic stories is that of Dan Jansen, the now-retired American speed skater. Jansen was inspired by his older sister Jane, who died before she was ever able to see him skate in the Olympics. He was a phenomenal skater from the time he was young.

He set a junior world record in the 500-meter race at age sixteen. Then, in 1988, Jansen became the world sprint champion, which sent him to the winter Olympics that same year—favored to win the 500- and 1,000-meter races.

But when it was his turn to win, Jansen fell. Then he fell again. He left the Olympics that year without a medal—but with a US Olympic Spirit Award for his undeniable spirit and good attitude. When he came back to the winter Olympics in 1992, the same thing happened, and he left again without any medals. Can you imagine the devastation? During the next two years, Jansen was the only skater to break 36 seconds in the 500 meters and did so four times. Then, in 1994, he arrived at the winter Olympics for one last chance at a medal.

Jansen may have had self-doubt going against him, but he had one thing on his side: fans. People loved him. They were rooting for him. How could you not love a guy who was clearly the best at what he did and who kept taking his losses with grace and determination to do things differently next time?

As he prepared to race in 1994, the entire crowd leaned in. As far as the crowd was concerned, they were on the ice with him. They wanted him to win as if they wanted themselves to win. This was his moment. This was his time. The entire world knew it. And yet everyone wondered, was he going to be able to pull it off?

With the crowd shouting his name and holding signs and cheering him on, Jansen raced the 1,000-meter event that year. He pulled out ahead and knew the time he was up against was the fastest ever skated. The last half lap, Dan would mention later in an interview, was the hardest part of the race for him. Still, he stayed ahead of it. And when he came across the finish line, he looked up to realize he had finally done it. He had finally finished first. He finally had his Olympic gold medal.

The entire audience exploded with applause. How could they not? Our successes and failures are interwoven. When we finish first, we give others permission to do the same. Besides, it takes more than just the ability to win to become a winner. It takes someone who knows how to lose and win. It takes the character of someone who can carry himself or herself like a champion, no matter what. The only way to be that kind of winner is to earn it. Dan Jansen did just that. What about you?

Getting Up and Starting Over

I teach this concept to my kids—when you make a mistake, you don't give up. You get up and try again. You erase and start over. My son Maxx gets impatient sometimes when he's doing his homework, and he'll rush to an answer. When he realizes it's the wrong answer, he'll be frustrated with the fact that he has to erase it and try again. I just remind him, "This is all part of the process. You erase and you start again."

When I faced that devastating loss at my first Nationals, do you think I wanted to get up and keep trying? I had fallen five times. Five times. I asked my coach what he thought had happened. "I wish I had an explanation," he said, but the only explanation was that I had choked. He couldn't even give me any advice for how to improve. It was just a bad day, and I needed to try again.

You wouldn't think that that first competition would be the setup for what came later in my career. It's because failure doesn't define us. You'd never hear anyone give this advice to an aspiring Olympic athlete: "First you have to go to Nationals and fall five times in front of tens of thousands of people." But if I would have allowed those failures to be debilitating, I never would have achieved the success that came next.

The attitude has to be, "No matter what happens, no matter what failure looks like, no matter how many times I have to try, I'm not giving up."

This attitude toward setbacks has permeated every other part of my life. Later, when I was diagnosed with cancer, the fear was extraordinary. And then I realized that I was not going to let this setback be the end of me. I discovered I was stronger, more capable, more resilient than I ever imagined.

Sue Guild is a female skater from the 1980s who was diagnosed with leukemia and kept skating anyway. At one point she'd lost all her hair, so she wore a wig. When she was out on the ice for her long program, her wig started to come loose. So, in the middle of the program, she reached up and pulled the wig off her head and threw it to the side. She finished the program without it—and the entire audience erupted with applause. That's the kind of commitment it takes to finish first. Sheer will and determination to continue, no matter what gets in your way.

May we be the kind of culture that continues to celebrate that kind of courage and strength rather than people who water down true success by whitewashing failure.

Sometimes when I talk about failure, people will argue that their failures preclude them from success because the failures were so public. They got a DUI, or got a divorce, or had to declare bankruptcy, or whatever it is. When they say this, I always remind them that a public failure actually makes it easier to get up and try again. What other choice do you have? I don't know of any skater in the history of skating who fell down and just stayed there. Instead, you go, "Oops, messed up. My bad. I'm going to try again."

If your wig falls off, if you get an unexpected diagnosis, if you fall five times, if you have multiple business failures and a mental breakdown, if you get a divorce or a DUI—own it. As horrible as those things are, you have to find a way to say, "I made the wrong move," or "This was unexpected, but I'm going to turn it around, and it isn't going to keep me from where I'm trying to go."

I have come in dead last, and second to last, and third to last. I've battled cancer and three brain tumors. And I have already made the decision that nothing is going to keep me from getting up and trying again. Because of that, I've been able to enjoy some pretty remarkable victories. What will it take for you to make a decision that you're not going to give up, no matter what failure you face on the way?

Long Roads and Remarkable Comebacks

In 1993, the Buffalo Bills played the Houston Oilers in an NFL playoff game. By halftime, there was a 32-point deficit. The Bills were losing. To make matters worse, they were playing without their quarterback Jim Kelly. But the Bills did something most people don't choose to do when they are faced with failure. They never allowed themselves to believe they were out of the game. In fact, while it seemed like an impossible task, the Bills were convinced they could close this losing gap.

As the television announcer stated that day, the Bills would have to travel the long way to get back to the Super Bowl, but Buffalo wasn't afraid of the long way. In fact, the long way invigorated them. In the second half of the game and during a bit of overtime, the Bills secured a victory of 41 to 38—without their star player. This goes down as one of the most memorable moments in NFL history—all because a team was willing to take what seemed like a failure and get up and try again.

Failure makes things interesting. Before failure, the path to victory seems so clear. So simple. Maybe not easy, but simple. After failure, we get creative. Failure makes us more aware of our weaknesses. It clarifies our obstacles. It reminds us to keep our heads in the game to the very end because success is never a guarantee—no matter how close it seems. And it reminds us how serious we're going to have to be if we're going to finish first.

No place is this more apparent than in sports when a victory seems clear but then the "losing" team makes a winning comeback.

You know what sports team has the longest losing streak of any team in history? The Chicago Cubs. They went 108 years without winning a world championship. Then, in 2016, the Cubs played another team with a history of losing—the Cleveland Indians. One of them was going to end their drought. True to form, the Cubs put themselves in a hole, having to win out from a three-to-one game deficit. But they had the right attitude about failure. They pulled it out.

They won their fifth game, then the sixth, and finally the seventh to end the most famous drought in sports history. The entire crowd erupted with their victory. The Indians, having lost game seven in the World Series, will have to try for it again in another series.

A comeback story reminds us how powerful we are, how strong we are, how resilient we are, and how when you give the human spirit room to thrive and to finish first, it will. It's just a matter of time.

You don't have to be an athlete to be capable of a remarkable comeback. Robert Downey Jr. experienced a great deal of success early on in his career, including an Academy Award nomination for his performance in the film *Chaplin*. Then, between the years 1996 and 2004, as Downey struggled with an addiction to alcohol and drugs, he started experiencing all kinds of very public setbacks, including several arrests. Downey admitted on *Oprah* years later that what drove him to treatment for his addiction was simple. "When . . . you just lost your job, and your wife left you. Uh, you might want to give it a shot." It was failure that drove Downey to his ultimate comeback, his return to success.

Downey eventually went through treatment for his drug addiction. After returning to acting in 2004, Downey said about the decision to seek treatment for his addiction, "It's not that difficult to overcome these seemingly ghastly problems... what's hard is to decide to do it." He's right. Those who have suffered and overcome know this to be true. The hardest part of success is making the decision to do it. After that, nothing can stop you. Finishing first actually comes quite naturally.

Failure Is to Be Forgiven, Not Feared

Instead of being smothered by your failures, debilitated by them, defeated by them, if you can learn from them, you have a superpower. True winners have a healthy appetite for failure. Because without failure, success means nothing.

This, honestly, is why I fear for kids in this upcoming generation. We have completely shielded them from failure. We've made it too easy for them to win. When they lose a soccer tournament but they get a trophy anyway, what incentive do they have to try something different next time? What incentive do they have to always be questioning, "Is this the best I can do?"

As adults, it's vital that we teach kids to look at failure and say, "Okay, what did I learn?" Failure is not something to be feared but something to be cherished because it is always teaching us. Failure is the glue that held my career together.

Speaking of public failures and how they bolster our path to success, one of the most heartbreaking failures I've ever had to witness was that of my acquaintance and legendary golfer

Tiger Woods. I'll never forget getting the call about Tiger during his first public incident and just praying that this was something he could rise above. Quickly the drama was all over the news, and everyone was wondering what was going on.

Only a few weeks later, I was in a hospital bed during my medical adventures of 2010, and Tiger was playing in a tournament. Things weren't going well. He wasn't himself—we could all tell. The nurse who was administering my treatment stood there, watching the television with me. At one point he turned to me and said, "You know when Tiger will go back to golfing well?" I didn't say anything. After a few minutes he answered his own question.

"When he forgives himself," he said.

What a powerful statement. What will it take for you to forgive yourself for the mistakes you have made? Nobody sets out to fail. And yet we all do it. When we forgive ourselves for our mistakes, we give ourselves permission to be successful again. When we give ourselves permission to not be perfect, we stop dragging around the dead weight of guilt and fear and self-hatred. Then everything can shift. Then the whole world opens up to us. We can begin being the champions we've been all along.

Too Far Gone?

Maybe you feel that your failure is too far gone for any kind of comeback.

You may wonder if it's too late for you or if your failure is too big or impossible to overcome.

God never sees people as "too far gone." There are thousands of stories in the Scriptures that prove this to be true, but of all the stories, no one quite embodies it like Lazarus, whom Jesus raises from the dead.

Lazarus's friends are very concerned for the apparent failure he is up against. He is sick and isn't getting better, and so his sister goes to Jesus to ask if He will come heal him. They've seen Jesus perform healing, so this isn't new to them, but they've never seen Jesus raise anyone from the dead.

Jesus assures Mary and Martha that Lazarus's sickness will not end in death, but it quickly becomes clear that Lazarus is going to die. Jesus isn't going to make it to him in time for the healing. In the face of this apparently permanent failure, Jesus tells the disciples, "Lazarus is dead, and for your sake I am glad I was not there, so that you may believe" (John 11:14–15). Can you imagine? What a thing for Jesus to say. I'm glad I wasn't there to prevent this failure—because then you would have all missed the miracle that followed, and that miracle strengthens our faith. How can you let Jesus into the failure in your story so that He can strengthen your faith?

What comes next would be the final time in Scripture that Jesus brings someone back from the dead until His own resurrection a few chapters later. In this moment, Jesus teaches us the most important lesson we can learn about failure. Failure builds our faith. It strengthens our resolve. There is no such thing as "too far gone" because the bigger the failure, the bigger the opportunity for us to prove what we're made of and for our God to prove just how powerful He is.

What if we started looking at our failure this way, rather than seeing it as a reason to give up? Perhaps we would be done wasting our time and our potential worrying about our setbacks and how they disqualify us from finishing first and we would discover just how brave, resilient, and capable we have been all along.

CHAPTER 9

EDIT YOUR CRITICS

*The critics are always right. The only way
you shut them up is by winning.*

–CHUCK NOLL[1]

During that time in the late 1970s, when I started skating better than I had ever skated in my life, a judge told my coach, "It's really great Scott is doing so well, but you have to understand he's too short to be competitive internationally." Isn't it interesting how people we don't even know feel like they get to decide what we're capable of accomplishing? Isn't it even more amazing how often we believe them?

Critics will be at every turn, ready to steal your focus. Ready to get you off track. They'll tell you that you can't do what you're trying to do, that you're wasting your time, and that you'll never finish first. But they don't get to make that choice for you. Only you have the power to do that.

I'm not saying that you should ignore your critics. This is the approach our culture often takes to criticism, and I think it's a big mistake. Instead of ignoring your critics or listening to them, if you can edit them, you'll have an amazing competitive advantage. You'll be able to take something that would distract or derail most people and use it as leverage to help you get where you're trying to go. This is the strength of a champion.

When you learn to edit your critics, criticism suddenly goes from being a stumbling block to being an incredible tool for building character, improving your performance, and giving you the strength you need to finish first. It will take some practice, sure. But I have great news. You can use the criticism in your life right this minute to help you strengthen the muscle. Just like any muscle, repetition and training will get you where you are trying to go.

This is about character. What kind of person do you want to be? Are you going to be the kind of person who hides from conflict and criticism, or are you going to give yourself permission to live up to your full potential? Are you going to do the work to become strong enough to receive and filter criticism, so editing your critics becomes second nature, or are you going to let critics distract you from what you've already decided is most important?

If you choose what I think you will, suddenly the same critics who would have derailed you will become a powerful tool at your disposal, actually helping you advance your goals. They become one of the key assets in your journey to finishing first. All because you learned to edit your critics.

Why Criticism Hurts

After I had that great breakfast, after I realized I was ranked second in the world, I was in a position I hadn't really considered until that moment. There would be more focus and expectation for what I was going to do next. The pressure to perform at a higher level began that morning.

It's funny. This is exactly the place where we all fight and wish and pray and hope to be, and then we get there and start worrying. We worry we peaked too soon or that we got there by accident or that we won't be able to hold on to the title. We wonder what people are saying or thinking about us, and we start prepping for failure before it even happens. We give our critics so much power, when the truth is that all the power is inside of us. Who cares what a critic says or doesn't say? You have the power to say, "Not true," or "I will prove you wrong," or "No thank you, delete."

Since before I was born, no one in skating had held on to the world title for four years and won the Olympic gold medal, so I was feeling the pressure. I knew my greatest strength was a lack of weakness, and I felt like I had really shored up my weaknesses. Yet I could practically hear the question on everybody's mind after my first world championship title: Did he win too soon?

For me, one of the most challenging aspects of criticism is that there is always a little bit of truth to it. You've heard the phrase "There's always a bit of truth in teasing"? The same is true for criticism.

This is why it hurts so much. Because we always know there is a chance our critics could be at least partially right. It's our job to prove them wrong. It's our job to edit the story.

The problem is, research shows that negative comments have a greater impact than positive ones. They're stickier. In fact, we need about ten positive comments to counteract the negative ones, according to research conducted by Roy F. Baumeister and others. The doctoral students in the study noted that "bad" events—like criticism, failure, and other negative impressions—had deeper and longer-lasting effects than good ones. "The distress participants reported over losing some money was greater than the joy or happiness that accompanied gaining some amount of money."[2]

This is why we ask people to recount their most embarrassing moments rather than their proudest ones. The embarrassing ones are more memorable (and funnier). They stay with us for longer. No wonder criticism is so concerning to us all. It has the potential to derail us and distract us, not just when it happens but for a long, long time after.

And yet our very control over our critics comes in how we choose to edit the information they present to us. This is a winner's attitude: Only I get to decide how criticism is going to affect my attitude. At the end of the day, there's only one winner, and then there's everyone else. Those who choose to finish first act differently, live differently, and make different choices than "most" people. As for me, I'm making the choice to edit my critics.

Softening the Blow

Rick Reilly is a friend of mine who wrote for *Sports Illustrated* for many years. He wrote an article one time about some angry NFL cheerleaders who sent him handwritten complaint letters but dotted their i's with little hearts. He joked about how funny this was to see—an angry letter with sweet little hearts all over it. It makes it a little easier to take criticism if we think of it like that. Little hearts all over the criticism.

I've watched far too many skaters ignore helpful criticism because it's too hard for them to digest the information being offered through feedback. Nine judges score them low in the category of artistry; meanwhile, skaters are saying, "I'm truly comfortable with my level of artistry." They're ignoring the feedback. Either they think they're smarter than the judges, or they're spinning the truth because they know they cannot do better. The judges determine their fates. How shortsighted is this?

We live in a culture that calls everyone who disagrees with us a "hater." Don't get me wrong. Haters are out there. But not everyone who disagrees with you is a hater. What if some of your "haters" could be your most valuable allies? You can go ahead and just keep losing. You can ignore the feedback. That's fine. But if you do that, you may be doing it at your own expense.

We need to learn not to be afraid to listen to what our critics are trying to tell us. Instead, we can use it as leverage to make a change. We have to learn to say, "You're right. I'm always late. I'm going to get better at that." Or, "Yes, I'm disorganized, but I'm going to come up with a system and stick to it because I want to finish first. I'm tired of being second place or last place in my life all the time. I'm ready for something better."

Where do I lack and how can I make up for that lack? If we can answer this question, we can get better. We can improve enough to reach our next victory, and then our next victory, and then our next one. Before we know it, we've gone from being last in Novice Men to first in the world. We have inspired ourselves, have changed our whole lives, and get to inspire an entire generation around us.

Consider the Source

One of the very first principles I teach people about criticism is to consider the source. I tell my kids this all the time: consider the source. Not all sources are created equally. Is this the kind of person who tells the truth? Someone who wants other people to succeed? Someone who is fair? Someone who is knowledgeable about your field? If not, the source is not legitimate, and the criticism is tainted. Unless you want the character of the person criticizing you, don't pay too much attention to it.

The second thing to consider is your critic's motive. Of course, you can't always know this, but if we think about possible motives, it may help us to dismiss criticism that is not only unhelpful but that also may derail us from finishing first.

Is the motive to distract you? Control you? Exert authority? Keep you down? Prevent you from passing him or her? Simply to be mean? If any of these motives seem true about this person, what good could possibly come from paying attention to his or her criticism? Once you start paying attention to who is criticizing you, you find a good deal of your criticism to be inconsequential. Unimportant. Simply a distraction from what you're trying to do.

Here's another thing to consider about a critic. For every bit of attention you give a critic, you can't give that exact amount of attention to your program, your practice, the work it takes to win. Critics know this. So many critics keep doing what they're doing because it's working. It doesn't help them to win, but it keeps you from winning, which is enough for them. Do you have enough integrity to stand in the face of criticism and not be swayed?

The word *integrity* was originally an architecture term that referred to a building's ability to withstand the pressure of earthquakes, floods, rain, tornados, and other natural disasters. A building with integrity wouldn't be swayed by high winds. It was strong enough to stand firm, to stand in its purpose, regardless of what happened outside. That's integrity. Do you have integrity? Are you strong enough to stand in the face of high winds and never veer from your purpose?

This is a biblical principle, too. Scripture teaches that the most valuable words we can listen to are the words of Jesus. Matthew 7:24–27 says:

Therefore everyone who hears these words of mine and puts them into practice is like a wise man who built his house on the rock. The rain came down, the streams rose, and the winds blew and beat against that house; yet it did not fall, because it had its foundation on the rock. But everyone who hears these words of mine and does not put them into practice is like a foolish man who built his house on sand. The rain came down, the streams rose, and the winds blew and beat against that house, and it fell with a great crash.

If you listen to the words of God, you'll finish first in spite of your critics. Meanwhile, you'll provide safety, shelter, and inspiration for anyone watching you. This is the kind of character it takes to be a champion. It's worth it—not only because of what you'll achieve but also because of what you provide for others who are looking in.

The Critic in Your Mind

The biggest trouble with critics is that, most of the time, we're our own greatest critic. This is a universally understood concept—that you are your own harshest judge. So how do you get away from the voice of criticism when the voice is inside your head?

Where did this voice come from? So often the critic started outside but then moved inside. We rehearsed the outside voice for long enough that it became a part of us.

If you grew up with parents who said you were strong and could accomplish anything you set your mind to, you are much more likely to succeed than if your parents were constantly pointing out your failures.

I gave a speech at a prayer breakfast a few years ago and kept asking my audience, over and over again, "Who do you want to be? What do you want your life to be about?" You get to decide who you want to be. Not anyone else. Not your critics. Not the voice inside your head. You. And if you want to be the kind of person who paves the way for others, who overcomes impossible challenges, who sets the bar higher and higher, who wakes others up to the potential lying dormant in them, who unlocks and unleashes your own hidden and unimaginable potential, then nothing will stop you. Not even your own doubts.

Those who have the loudest inner critic also often become the most relentless critics of those around them. This is a hidden danger of giving in to your inner critic. Suddenly you become the one pointing out everyone else's faults, making it impossible—or at least extra challenging—for anyone to reach his or her full potential.

You have suddenly become the one asserting your supposed authority, trying to keep people down, distracting them from the work they're doing to reach new heights. Here's something to remember. Winners are rarely big critics. It's not that they're not discerning. It's just that they're not wasting time looking around at everyone else, trying to correct their mistakes. They're too focused for that. They're too busy. They're too interested in pointing people toward what is possible, rather than dragging them down with useless criticism.

If you allow yourself to be overly critical of others, you will drag yourself down. You'll be frozen and stuck. There's no way to be a big critic and also be a champion. Bob Goff famously said, "Most people need love and acceptance a lot more than they need advice."

I think this is so true. May we be winners.

But may we be the kind of winners who focus more on the best in people than the worst in them. Including, especially, ourselves.

Opinions Versus Information

The information you get from your critics is simply that: information. Data. No need to be emotional about this. It's just feedback. The problem is, it's really hard to get pure information these days. When it comes to critics, almost all information is biased.

Information from your opponent is biased, but so is information from your grandmother. To have any usable data from your critics, you either need better sources or are really good at sifting through the bias to find the information that will help you succeed.

We recently had a conversation with the kids about how not all information is created equally. We were all watching the news one night and I told them, "The minute you hear someone say 'I think,' turn off the television. Or change the channel." Because what do we care what this person thinks? Why is what he or she thinks more important than what you think? If it's not information, it's not news, and it's not important. It's not helpful. What we're looking for is information. Information can help us win.

What distinguishes information from opinion is that there is no judgment to it. "You ran that mile thirty seconds slower than your average." There's information. "You are too short to win." There's opinion. One can be used to improve. The other is going to alter your state of being. It's going to affect your mood, stay in your memory, and prevent you from performing well next time. Well, next time has nothing to do with this time.

We have to get over this tendency we have to make positive or negative judgments over one bad day, one bad performance, one weak moment, one supposed failure. Your critics will love to linger on these things. You can't allow yourself to linger there with them.

"Who said that I am to be measured by how well I do things?" W. Timothy Gallwey, author of *The Inner Game of Tennis*, reminds us. "In fact, who said that I should be measured at all?" He goes on to talk about how bending to this idea will derail us from our objectives and that to disengage from this trap we must gain a clear knowledge that "the value of a human being cannot be measured by performance—or by any other arbitrary measurement."

Whether you win or lose, whether today is your best or

worst, this has nothing to do with your value as a human. It's simply information. The better we can get at this, the more likely we are to win. The more likely we are to become the kind of person we've always known ourselves to be—someone capable of overcoming incredible challenges in order to get what we most want.

The minute we can start to edit down our criticism and get to the information, that's the minute we can use it to our advantage. It's not about where you are today; it's about where you're going to be. We have to remind ourselves: This is where I am, but it is not where I'm always going to be. The quality of your life has to do with where you're getting your information.

Write Your Own Story

My critics said that no one could hold on to the title of national champion for four years, but I chose to write my own story. I went four years undefeated—didn't lose a single competition from October 1980 until March 1984. As for the judge who told me I was too short to be competitive internationally, I wasn't interested in his story about me. So I went on to take the Olympic gold for male figure skaters in 1984. Just like that, I edited my critics. I wrote my own story.

Criticism can either be a debilitating distraction or it can be a tool you use to your advantage. Either way, no matter what kind of criticism comes in, I have learned over time to let it come and let it go. To let the pendulum swing as it will.

Things will be great for a while. Then they will be not so great. Then they will be great again. But if I live my life constantly trying to control the criticism that comes in or out, I'll make myself miserable.

This doesn't have to be dramatic. It can just be about tuning my ears and being picky about what information I choose to let linger. If you're on a path, if you're on track to take your life to a place you never thought it could go before, you can't let criticism derail you. You just can't. It's not worth it. You just have to stay on your track. Nobody gets to decide your future except for you.

CHAPTER 10

PLAY BY THE RULES OF THE GAME

*Character cannot be developed in ease
and quiet. Only through experience of trial
and suffering can the soul be strengthened,
ambition inspired, and success achieved.*

—HELEN KELLER[1]

There was a thunderstorm in Nashville last night, and our house got hit by lightning. This has happened before, but this time it took out our junction box, which is like the central nervous system of the house. So while two of my kids were at their after-school activities, two were at home trying to figure out what they were going to do without television or video games.

I walked around the house with the repair guy, trying to figure out exactly what was wrong and what needed to be fixed. Meanwhile, I heard my nine-year-old son and my thirteen-year-old daughter talking about how they were going to pass the time. Maxx, my nine-year-old, finally asked his sister, "Do you want to play Monopoly?"

Now, to really understand the setup of this, you have to get that Evelyne is from Haiti and her first language is Creole. She does really well with English but is still learning and certainly didn't grow up playing Monopoly. So imagine a nine-year-old who doesn't know how to play Monopoly teaching a thirteen-year-old who speaks English as a second language how to play. It was like the blind leading the blind.

I spent some time eavesdropping on their conversation and realized that, as little as they knew about the game, they were at least having a good time. They weren't playing the game correctly—didn't know the rules and, therefore, had no idea how to know when someone had won the game—but they were playing joyfully nonetheless.

At one point I poked my head through the door and said, "Hey, guys, next time you play Monopoly, I'll have to play with you so I can teach you the rules of the game." They both looked at me like I was crazy. "Dad, we don't need you to teach us. We know what we're doing." I watched them for a little bit longer and smiled to myself. They weren't even using the hotels or houses, and neither of them had any strategy for what they were doing.

Not only did they not know how to play the game correctly, but they also didn't really want to know. This is the beauty of being a kid. They could play with joy, regardless of the fact that they were doing it wrong.

The whole thing made me think about how there is a time in life when you can do this—you can find joy in all kinds of things without having to know the rules of the game. You can find joy in just doing it, just passing the time. But later, when you become a little bit more mature, you realize that you want your efforts to actually mean something. You want them to be taking you somewhere. You want to invest in something that is actually going to pay you back.

This is the moment when we go from just fiddling around with our lives to actually taking ourselves seriously. We start to act like a champion, look like a champion, dress like a champion, carry ourselves like a champion, and win like a champion. In doing that, we raise the bar for ourselves and everyone around us.

If you're a nine-year-old and a thirteen-year-old passing time on a night when the power is out, it's okay not to know the rules of the game. It's even a little cute. Endearing. But if you're ready for something more meaningful than that, then it's time to become a winner. If you've been reading this book and feel like something is tugging at your soul, it's time to start living with more intention. It's time to figure out what it would look like for you to win.

Life as a Game

In Monopoly, I'm unbeatable if I'm the car. Not so much if I'm the hat or the boot, but if I'm the car, watch out. And the key to winning Monopoly, if you ask me, is to buy St. James Place, Tennessee Avenue, and New York Avenue—the orange properties right before the free parking.

They're not the properties most people usually go for, but they're the cheapest properties to build on later in the game, so I always buy them early on.

Next, I always go for the purple spaces: St. Charles Place, Virginia Avenue, and so on. If you can secure these two little corners of the Monopoly board, you basically have the rest of the game in the bag. I would say more, but in case I ever play you in Monopoly, I'm going to stop. The point is, when you've played a game enough times and when you really know the rules, you can come up with a winning strategy.

What if you turned everything you did in your life into a game? Let's say you want to get out of debt. What if you turned that into a numbers game? Or, if you want to get a college scholarship, why not think of it like a board game—such as Monopoly? What are the rules to getting a college scholarship, and how can you use those rules to your advantage? What are the pieces you would need to move around to get where you're trying to go? How can you be unbeatable at this thing you're trying to do?

I've had the opportunity to spend some time with Donny Osmond and always enjoyed his enthusiasm. I saw a profile of him on television where his kids were talking about his parental approach. His thinking was, "If anything is unpleasant, we'll make it into a game. You can transform anything by making it a game."

All that means is asking yourself, What does success look like in this endeavor? What are the steps it's going to take for me to get there? How do I begin taking some of those steps?

If you're trying to get a college scholarship, you'll need to find out what the requirements are for securing the scholarship. Do you need a 3.8 GPA? Do you need a certain score on your SATs or ACTs? Do you need a certain number of community service hours? From there, you can build a pretty solid to-do list and just begin chipping away. Begin to play by the rules of the game and you'll be shocked by how quickly doors open for you.

How did I go from being a last-place skater to being an Olympic gold medalist? It's the same way I got really good at Monopoly. I figured out the rules to the game and created a step-by-step process for myself to get where I was trying to go. I didn't allow myself any excuses. I didn't let my fear of failure get in the way. I just knew what I needed to do, and I did it.

Whether you want to be a spelling bee champion, win your bowling league, or be the president of the United States, it can all be broken down to the rules of the game. Like Monopoly. You can do the same thing if you want to be a successful speaker, or if you want to get into medical school, or if you want to publish a bestselling book. You start by playing the game and then pay attention to the feedback you get.

Are you winning the game? If not, how can you improve? If you are, what are you doing that is helping you to win and how can you strengthen these skill sets to make yourself unbeatable? If success is a journey, your character is revealed in the process. Deep down we are all strong. But are you living up to your true identity?

Develop a Champion's Character

I mentioned my friend Mike Eruzione earlier in the book. Mike started playing hockey at a young age. He dreamed like most young kids of what life would be like after high school, and he pictured himself going to the University of New Hampshire, playing his three favorite sports: baseball, football, and hockey. But as most plans do, his fell through, and Mike ended up making plans to head to the smaller and lesser-known Merrimack College, a Division II school.

Then in July, the summer before he started at Merrimack, he got a call from a friend, asking him to play for a summer league. Typically he didn't play hockey in the summer, but he agreed, thinking maybe it would be a good way to stay in shape. And, miracle of all miracles, a guy who happened to be refereeing one of the games Mike played that summer was Jack Parker, the assistant coach at Boston University.

Mike showed up and played like he usually did. He wasn't trying to impress anyone. He didn't even know there was anyone to impress. He just brought the same intensity to the ice that he always brought, the same work ethic he carried with him wherever he went. The work ethic of a champion. And when the summer league ended, Jack asked Mike if he would be interested in a scholarship to Boston University.

One "yes" to a summer league, one commitment to play your heart out even though it is only a pickup game, one choice to bring your winning self to the table even when you're not sure it will matter, can change everything. You never know when that opportunity will come. You may not even recognize it when it gets there. For now, you just have to be willing to make the choice. You get to decide if you want to be the kind of person who finishes first.

Mike played the rest of his career at Boston University. As always, he put in the work. He became the second-all-time leading scorer for the university and was drafted by the Hartford Whalers. And yet when it came time to sign a pro contract, he was sent to Toledo to play as an amateur.

This didn't discourage Mike. Instead, he kept playing his heart out. At the end of his first season, he was voted outstanding American-born player of the year. He was certain he would sign with the New York Rangers and turn pro. But right as his time was coming, the general manager of the team, John Ferguson, was fired. And the new manager wasn't interested in signing any of Ferguson's guys.

As quickly as it had come, the opportunity he thought was his was yanked from underneath him. You may have been in a position like this, where it seemed as though everything was coming together and then it all fell apart. The decision you make in this moment—to act like a champion or to complain and play the victim—determines everything. As for Mike, he chose to act like the champion he is, to go back to Toledo as an amateur.

It was in Toledo that Mike made the decision to try out for the famous 1980 Olympic hockey team. If everything had gone exactly as he had planned, Mike Eruzione never would have been on the US Olympic hockey team that year. He never would have won his gold medal. He never would have been a part of the "Miracle on Ice," as it was called. Even more important, if Mike had not made the decision early on to live as a winner, act as a winner, and play as a winner, he never would have found himself standing on the gold medal platform. Winning is a choice. You get to decide.

We do not get to choose all of the opportunities that come our way. We do not get to choose our entire path. But we do get to choose what to do with setbacks and opportunities that come our way. We do get to choose how we behave as we wait to know what is coming next. We do get to decide that no matter what happens, we will be ready. Are you willing to have a good attitude even when things aren't going your way? This is the attitude of a winner.

Establish Your Trustworthiness

I have this weird hobby of collecting life-threatening illnesses. Due to that, I've had to live differently if I wanted to live at all. This means that I've developed habits of eating healthfully, working out, and thinking positively because if I didn't, it would cost me more than it costs most people. These things are simple. Avoiding sugar. Getting my workouts in every day.

Drinking enough water. Reading my Bible. None of the habits are too dramatic, but they have an amazing effect when you do them all together.

I tell the skaters I work with, "If you want to be competitive, you're not allowed to miss in the short program." What I mean is that, of the seven elements you're required to hit in the short program, you're not allowed to miss on any of them. Not one, ever. This consistency is the equivalent, in my mind, of drinking your water and doing your exercises and reading your Bible. You simply can't miss. Not even one.

You have to build a reputation with the judges that you take even the small things seriously. That you won't miss. When you build that kind of relationship with the judges, over time they come to expect and appreciate that you are the kind of skater who delivers, no matter what.

You win in the small things, which helps you to win in the big ones.

It's no different in the business world. Business deals are not made in a single interaction. They're made over the course of time. It's conversation after conversation, business meeting after business meeting, e-mail exchange after e-mail exchange. This is all part of building trust with a client. If they know you are trustworthy with e-mail, they can assume you are going to deliver for them on deadlines. If you're trustworthy with the small things, you'll be trustworthy with the big ones.

Trust isn't built in one interaction or two or three. It's built in the day-to-day moments of life. Victories build on each other. Have you stopped to ask yourself what would make today a win for you? You don't need to hit all of your goals today. You may only need to accomplish one small goal—and that can be the victory you stand on tomorrow to accomplish your next small goal. Small victories empower us for bigger victories.

Those who win in the big things are faithful in the small things. If you believe finishing first is about being big and flashy, when it's really about showing up and doing the work, you will miss it.

Behave with Humility

Too many champions get stuck in the trap of winning for the wrong reasons. I never wanted that to be me. I never wanted to be the kind of guy other people were rooting against. I never wanted to be the opponent other people wanted to bring down. I always wanted to be the guy who was so nice, he was impossible to hate. I am the type of person who wants to be liked, and I wasn't going to let competition change that about me.

For some, winning is about sticking out their chest and rubbing their competitors' noses in their greatness. For me, winning has always been about something bigger. That mission has been so important to me. So every time there was a crack in the door, I took it. I did my part as best I could. But I never allowed myself to get too attached to the outcome. I wanted to win. But I wasn't willing to step on people in the process.

The other thing I did was to make the choice that I was going to be the kind of person who wasn't afraid to get his hands dirty. Even after my Olympic success, my attitude was, "Okay, you need me to unload trucks? I'll unload trucks. You need me to do a media interview at 5:00 a.m. even though my plane landed at 2:00 a.m.? I'll do it." If I didn't succeed, it was never going to be because I didn't do my part.

Take Risks

One of the reasons I've been so successful with my yearly charity event—An Evening with Scott Hamilton and Friends—is because I'm not afraid to take chances. Every year I do something drastically different. Something nobody is expecting. Something people can't help but talk about. They might not even necessarily like what I do, but they can't help but talk about it. What does the audience like? What surprises and delights them? How can I get them on their feet next time?

It's easy for me to do this because usually the event is not about me. When your goal is bigger than you and you realize, in fact, so little of what you do is about you, that no one is paying much attention to you anyway, suddenly you can get out of your own way. If you're struggling with getting out of your own way, ask yourself who needs this that is not you. Do it for that person.

After recovering from my first brain tumor—which took away all pituitary function and left me taking medications for total hormone replacement—I knew I had a lot of work to do if I was ever going to be in good physical shape again. I had stopped skating shortly before the tumor presented itself and had gained weight from both the radiation and the drugs I was required to take. So I was twenty-five pounds heavier than I was used to being.

After the ninth anniversary of my annual cancer benefit in Cleveland, I decided I would come back to skating for the tenth anniversary show. I knew it was going to be hard. I was older than I had ever been (surprising, right?) and had all of these physical obstacles I needed to overcome. But I also knew I wouldn't be satisfied with myself if I didn't go for it. So I made the decision to get back on the ice.

Shortly after I decided this, I ran into my friend Tom Petersson of the band Cheap Trick, whom I've known for more than twenty-five years. I told Tom I was ready to get back on the ice and that I wanted him to be onstage during my first show back. As soon as I said it out loud, I knew there was no going back. It is powerful to tell someone what you're trying to do because now you're accountable.

I reached out and contacted my trainer, Francis Fessler, to tell him what I was trying to do. I told him I needed his help to get in shape. He set up a training regimen designed to help me build strength and flexibility and avoid injury, as well as drop weight, then get me on the ice. It was a slow and steady plan. Just showing up, day after day. For now.

After a few months of working out, I asked my choreographer, Sarah Kawahara, to help with a routine for my first night back on the ice. She agreed and came to meet me, but when she watched me skate, I was not expecting her response. She said, "This is it? This is as far as you've come? This isn't acceptable, Scott." Sarah told me that if I wanted to skate again, I had to do better. She choreographed a routine, but it was one she knew would stretch me further than I had been able to go, up to that point.

This was a wake-up call for me. Honestly, it was the realization that showing up every day and doing things little by little was good but wasn't enough to be a champion. If I wanted to be a champion, I was going to have to work harder than that. I was going to have to outwork everybody.

At that point the workouts from Francis took on another trait: torturous. I kept showing up every day in mind, body, and spirit, but now I had to bring something else with me. Iron will. A willingness to suffer temporary pain for a long-term gain.

These are the moments when you wonder if it is all worth it. But I would remind myself, what else was I going to do besides continue to suffer? To suffer the pain of being average, to suffer the knowledge that there was more I could do and I was hiding my potential.

It took time, but I started to do okay. The hard work I was putting in at the gym was showing up on the ice. I was doing some double jumps, getting my legs back under me. I was starting to get in the air and starting to spin a little. After all my hard work, I had achieved the skill level of a really average juvenile skater.

Be Memorable

A few weeks before the big event, I found myself in a New York City cab with my friend Bobby Goldwater, a former executive at Madison Square Garden as well as the Staples Center in Los Angeles. We had been friends for years, and I told him what I was doing. He listened and nodded knowingly. Then, when I finished, he asked, "So, are you going to do a backflip?" I turned to look at him in that cab as we inched through the crowded streets of New York City. A skeptical smile came over my face.

"Are you crazy?" I said. "I'm fifty-one years old. The last thing I need to be doing is backflips on the ice."

He nodded but also shrugged. "Don't you think there is going to be some expectation? I mean, when was the last time you did a show without a backflip?"

Suddenly, as we sat there in that cab, I realized what I needed to do—regardless of whether it seemed crazy. People were going to be expecting me to do a backflip. This was the expectation I had set. And, yes, it was unexpected for a fifty-one-year-old figure skater to do a backflip, but that was all the more reason I was going to do one.

I called Francis right away and told him I needed to do a backflip. He wasn't surprised and found a guy named Tim

Richards, owner of Let It Shine Gymnastics, which was really close to the rink, and Tim said he could help me.

So he set me up with a program—we started practicing on a soft trampoline, then a little bit harder of a trampoline, then a little bit harder, then a tumbling run, and then a gymnastics floor.

He didn't spare me any pain. He wanted me doing as many as sixty backflips in a day, and I came as close to that as I possibly could, even when I was getting sick. I was determined and knew that if I wanted to do something extraordinary, I had to act in extraordinary ways.

When I finally decided to take the backflip to the ice, I started with two spotters on either side of me—with a rope tied around my waist so they could catch me if anything happened. Then I removed one of the spotters, then the other spotter, and before I knew it, I was doing backflips on the ice again. At that point I knew I had it. I was feeling crazy but also like, "I've got this thing."

This is the power of hard work. You suddenly realize you can do things you never thought you could do. You have power you never knew you had.

There are endless stories of people who have been told, "You can't, you won't, you shouldn't . . ." and who have overcome all the odds to do it anyway. Will you be one of those people? When you know who you are and what you are capable of achieving, why would you not finish first? Unrealized potential is some of the greatest pain in the world.

If you are suffering or hurting, there is a way out—work

hard. We are wired for hard work. Some of our greatest pain in life is because we are avoiding work. Build your life in the way of a champion. Be memorable. Be unique. Be different. Be special. Be the absolute best version of you.

We get only one shot at this thing called life. If you're not satisfied, there is a reason. It's time to stop sitting around wasting time, waiting for what you want your life to be like; it's time to start going after the amazing things you know are possible for you. It's time to begin realizing the unique potential that has always been waiting for you.

Put Everything on the Line

When I arrived in Cleveland to do my backflip on the ice in front of an audience for the first time, I was ready. Or so I thought. Eight thousand people waited in the audience, not sure what to expect from me, wondering what my comeback would look like.

I made it through my first program without a problem, which was shorter and simpler than the longer program. Then it came time to do my big solo near the end of the show that would feature my backflip. I got out on the ice and went for it—giving it everything I had. Cheap Trick was singing the song "Miracle," and I went for my first jump, and the weirdest thing happened. I just sat down. Fell all the way to the ground.

Even stranger than the fall was when I started to get up; I realized my legs were just gone—totally wasted from all those workouts. All the hard work I had put in to do this backflip and now I wasn't sure I could even manage it. To land this thing, I'd have to get up, power skate all the way down to the other end of the ice, and come back to where I was now to execute the flip. I lifted myself off the ice and thought to myself, *I'm doomed.*

But I took a half circle around the ice to get some speed open, and as I skated across the center of the ice to the other end of the rink, I looked square into the face of William Shatner. I burst out laughing. And that moment broke the tension for me. I thought, *Now, there's something you don't see every day.* The fact that William Shatner was sitting there, watching me skate, made me feel like he was there to support me in this quest. We have been great friends for a very long time.

So I skated as hard as I possibly could toward the other end of the rink, and I gave every last ounce of energy I had, and I threw the backflip. At that point there were about forty seconds left in my routine, but as soon as I landed the backflip, the entire arena stood to its feet and stayed standing for the remainder of my routine. The audience got me through that performance.

That was when I realized that none of this had ever been about skating. It was about pushing past my limitations. It was about demonstrating—for myself and that entire audience—what was possible. It was about inspiring others to explore the limits of what was possible for them. This is why eight thousand people stood in an arena. Not because I did a backflip but because I just showed them what is possible when we're willing to push beyond our own self-imposed limitations.

That was one of the most powerful moments I've had on the ice in my entire skating career. And it happened for me at fifty-one. Age is never an excuse. Physical limitations are never an excuse. It's never too late. It's never too early, either.

Are you willing to swallow your pride and do whatever it takes to get your audience on its feet? Are you willing to get over your own ego and try something truly different, something revolutionary, something even a little drastic to get out of your comfort zone and make an impact? If what you've tried hasn't worked, try something else. Be the person who raises the bar. Do it for yourself or do it for someone else, but more importantly, do it because it makes the world a better place.

Not too long after I landed that flip, the brain tumor came back for a second time, and I realized there was a second reason to be in good shape, beyond the fact that I could do a backflip on ice skates. My strong physical condition was going to help me survive. There are a million reasons to finish first—and zero reasons to talk yourself out of it. At least no good ones. Are you ready yet to get started?

Listen for the Applause

I skated with the Ice Capades for a while, and its president Dick Palmer was someone whom I respected immensely. He was a guy who knew how to play by the rules of the game. Do you know how he evaluated his skaters? He would stand in the mezzanine and listen to the applause. If a skater could get a great reaction from the crowd, that skater was invaluable to him. If a skater couldn't, he needed to get someone in there who could make that happen. Those were the rules of the game.

What would it look like for you to stand in the mezzanine of your life and listen to the kind of applause you're getting? Where are you getting the audience on its feet, and where do you have room to improve?

Whether you're playing Monopoly or tennis or trying to start a business, winning and losing provide incredible feedback. Whether you're ice skating, trying to secure a top job, or launching a new product, you have to pay attention to how others are responding to what you're doing. Feedback is a reliable indicator of your progress.

Everything I've given you up to this point is the foundation for what you're about to do, which is to start building your dream life. You get to decide where you're trying to go—what success means to you. Nobody gets to decide that for you. And once you've decided, you have no reason not to really go for it. To play like a grown-up, to become the champion you have always been.

NEVER LOOK BACK

Winning is fun . . . sure. But winning is not the
point. Wanting to win is the point. Not giving up
is the point. Never letting up is the point. Never
being satisfied with what you've done is the point.

—PAT SUMMITT[1]

For a long time, finishing first felt like it was all about being a competitive skater. I didn't have any clue at the time that I would do work with cancer, that I would open the Scott Hamilton Skating Academy, or that I would tour for so long with Stars on Ice. I was focused on one victory at a time.

Inevitably my competitive skating career came to an end, and I started my professional skating career. When I toured with Stars on Ice, my life didn't become any less competitive, but the competition started to shift. I was focused on how we could grow as performers and as a team, how we could continually create a culture of excellence, and how we could set the bar higher and higher for the audience each year. I wanted to keep surprising our audience with everything we did.

Every time I performed, I'd look down in the audience and inevitably see a guy sitting next to his wife, checking his watch, looking miserable. I realized what was happening— probably—was that his wife had requested to go to the ice show for date night. He complied, praying that none of his friends would see him there.

I knew in my heart it was my job to entertain that guy. To win him over. If I could get him on his feet, if I could earn his respect, he would not mind coming back again, and I could keep skating for as long as it was fun for me. What I realized is that I was skating for people who didn't want to be there as much as I was skating for those who did and that the greatest compliment I could ever be given would be to get everyone on their feet.

Especially the guy who didn't want to be there.

Even today I will be in an airport somewhere and a man will walk up to me and ask if I'm "that skater." I respond "yes," of course, and then he tells me he doesn't watch skating—he's more of a football or basketball guy—but that his wife absolutely loves me. Then he goes to get his wife and brings her back and says, "Look who I found!" and she has absolutely no idea who I am.

When this happens, every single time I say to myself, "I win." This is the power of continually pushing to be better.

I used to say to the other skaters, "If everybody is going to do a butt wiggle and a triple toe loop, we're not going to stay in business very long." In other words, we need to be constantly setting the bar higher. We can't rest on our past successes. We can't be satisfied with what we did back then. We always, always have to be pushing forward to what is in front of us. And in doing that, we make ourselves an appreciating asset instead of a depreciating one, living off of our past successes.

Success can be its own obstacle if we're not careful. Too many of us hold on to our past wins at the expense of future wins. If you're dwelling in the past—even the really good stuff about your past—there is no way you'll ever make any progress in your life. It's like eating half an apple and thinking you'll save the rest for later. The more time that goes by, the less appealing the apple looks. Stale success is like a browned apple.

What served us today won't necessarily serve us tomorrow. What was nourishing yesterday becomes poisonous if we're always stashing it away, saving it for later. This is why I hid my Olympic gold medal in my underwear drawer for so long. I didn't want any reason to get stuck in the past. As amazing as that moment of victory was, I didn't want to stay there. I always want to be changing and growing.

You will move the direction in which you're pointed. If you are always looking back to the past, reliving your failures or even your successes, no wonder you're not moving forward very quickly. You can either spend time sitting around, thinking about the "glory days," or you can get about the business of finishing first in your life right now. The idea is to stay pointed forward, to focus your attention on the direction you'd like to go.

Focus Forward

One key way I have been able to stay focused forward is by setting my eyes on people who are better, faster, stronger, and more confident than I am. It's hard to get too confident in yourself when you've surrounded yourself with people who are all better than you in one form or another.

One of my very favorite skaters to watch when I was young was Gordon McKellen—Gordie, as we called him. He was the three-time national champion and the best show skater I had ever seen in my life. When Gordie walked into a room, two things would happen. First, someone would put Neil Diamond on because this was his favorite music. And, second, women would all fix their hair and everyone would move their chairs closer so they could talk with him. I mean, who doesn't want to have that kind of pull? It was magnetic.

Watching Gordie gave me permission. That was the biggest thing I got from him. He was fearless, and watching him take chances gave me permission to take my own chances in skating, to try new things and be exactly the kind of skater I wanted to be. I wasn't exactly like him. But I didn't need to be. I could take the elements of his fight and drive that inspired me so much and use them as fuel to become my own best version of myself. That's what Gordie did for me.

He gave me permission to be the skater I had always wanted to be.

Another skater who always kept me facing forward was a Russian pairs skater named Irina Rodnina. The thing I admired most about Irina was that she always won. I mean always. It wasn't that when she stepped on the ice people thought she could win. It was that they assumed she would win. When she was competing, we would all think to ourselves, *Okay, who's skating for second?*

Part of the reason I liked her so much was because she was everything that I wasn't. She was confident. She was strong. She skated fast. She had all the qualities I didn't have but that I wished I had. We need people like this in our line of sight—people who represent the qualities we want to have but haven't been able to achieve yet. They remind us that the unthinkable is possible. We point ourselves in their direction, and we move in the direction we're pointed.

Irina won ten world titles and three Olympic gold medals with two different partners. Not only that, but as a pairs skater, she also always made her partners better. She called them to the highest standard, sometimes even higher than they themselves thought they could reach. When she and her partner would go out on the ice, it was almost like she was daring her partner to skate even faster. She was a fierce competitor, a force to be reckoned with.

If you don't have people you admire like that—who you consider heroes, who remind you of what's possible, and who point you toward your greatest potential—it's time to get some. A big part of my success in skating came because my heroes weren't skaters. I admired anyone who would build a platform over time. Look around you. Look for the people who are having the kind of impact you want to have. You won't have to look far.

Stop Living As If You Have a Shelf Life

The attitude of finishing first has to be, "Who I am today is not who I want to be. It's the foundation of who I am becoming." This applies not only to my skills in my industry but also to my character and integrity.

When I turned pro and started doing Stars on Ice, the one thing guiding my vision was that I knew I needed to build an audience. I had watched so many other athletes be successful for a relatively short period of time and then not do much after, and I knew I didn't want to do that.

I don't know about you, but I don't want to have a shelf life. I don't want to expire. I always want to be leveraging the success I have toward a greater impact. My vision has always been so much bigger than skating. I always want to have my eyes on the horizon of where I'm going, what I'm going to do next.

But the thing I realized about building an audience is that you can't do it simply by being a great athlete. You have to be a remarkable person. If you're great at skating, or basketball, or playing the piano, you'll get a few people to follow you. But it isn't until you prove who you are as a person that the world begins to take notice. Once you've become the best in your field, what are you going to do next?

Think about Neil Diamond for a minute. Whether you're a die-hard fan of his music or not, you know who he is. That's because Diamond doesn't just perform his music. He touches your heart. He isn't just a good guitar player. He builds a relationship with people. He wins them over. He shares the joy of his music, and everyone who listens is always happy they did. If we can do that, it doesn't really matter if we're doing it through music or skating or ventriloquism. Making people smile is really what it's all about.

That's what I set out to do with Stars on Ice. I wanted to make people smile.

When you make the decision to do this, you become different and special. This attitude is so unique that it gets people's attention. It is easy for someone to show up and act like, "Look, I've worked really hard and already accomplished a lot. More than most of you. It's time for you to worship me." But that's not the kind of person I want to be, and I know it's not the kind of person you want to be, either.

I just watched Neil Diamond perform his 50 Year Anniversary World Tour. Can you believe that? Fiftieth anniversary. How many of us can say we've been doing something for fifty years—and not just doing it, but doing it in a way that is so full of contagious joy, it's drawing audiences from all over the world? This is what Diamond is doing, and no wonder he's a legend. I want to be the kind of person who spreads joy and hope the way he does.

What kind of person do you want to be? Do you want to be the kind of person who rests in what you did "back then" or the kind of person who is always pushing yourself toward your next greatest achievement? Do you want to be the kind of person who has one moment of glory in your life or the kind of person who consistently delivers results and spreads contagious joy wherever you go?

You can hold on to your past successes, but if you do, you'll never discover the hidden potential living inside you. Face forward, focus forward, and ask yourself how you can use every experience you've had as a building block to become the person you have purposed yourself to become.

Be Willing to Do Something Badly

When it comes to karaoke, if there is one guy who could skip it, that would be me. The audience might even appreciate if I did. But think of all the fun I would miss if I didn't let myself be bad at something every now and then. Some things are worth doing even if we do them badly.

Many years ago, I found myself at Garry Shandling's house after playing golf with my friend Kevin Nealon. Kevin and I had met a few years before at the White House. President Bush had invited athletes and entertainers to a sports day on the south lawn, and while I was there, we became friends. My kids call him Big Kevin because he is six foot five. We were the two shyest people at the event, so we gravitated toward each other.

At Garry's house that day, it was like celebrity central, which can make you feel like you don't want to do anything to draw attention to yourself. So when Garry suggested we all play a game of basketball, I hesitated. I looked around the court and realized I was the shortest person there. But then I thought, *You know, I might be the worst player here, but it will be fun.* So I played, and I'm so glad I did. It's a memory I'll carry with me for the rest of my life.

You don't have to be the best at everything. You can decide to do something just because it's fun or because someone you love likes to do it or because you want to. Take a deep breath and launch. Give something a try. Don't take yourself so seriously. You never know what might happen.

On my fiftieth birthday, as a gift, David Fishof, the owner of the Rock 'n' Roll Fantasy Camp, gifted me a spot at one of his camps. It had always been a dream of mine to play the drums, and I figured this was my chance. So I started taking lessons a little bit, and I told my friend Sterling Ball what I was doing. The next thing I knew, a drum set showed up on my front porch. So I spent a little bit of time playing alone in my house, practicing here and there, making some progress. By the time I showed up at the fantasy camp, I felt like I was ready.

But, of course, the minute I started looking around, I realized I was surrounded by legends. I saw Danny Seraphine, the original drummer for Chicago, and Alan White, the drummer for Yes. My heroes. I'm not joking when I say I was, basically, paralyzed with fear. On the very first note I hit on my drums, both of my sticks flew out of my hands. I almost died.

Instead, I told myself, "Well, now that the worst has happened, it's all uphill from here . . . time to have some fun."

There's something freeing about not being the best at something. There's something really great about saying, "I'm going to give this a shot, no matter how it goes."

Rami Jaffee, the keyboard player for the Wallflowers, was the camp counselor assigned to bring us together as a band. He helped us choose an Aerosmith song that we would perform at the end of camp at the Whiskey a Go Go. We went to work practicing, five total strangers and my friend Bob Fishman, the CBS Sports television director. Even though we didn't know what we were doing, we were willing to learn how to play that classic song together, to give it justice.

To top it off, the band also had to perform for a private showing. Sooner than later, the legends began to walk in. Songwriter and producer Bill Hudson. Rock drummer Sandy Gennaro. Then the one and only lead singer of Aerosmith, Steven Tyler! I just sat there, a beginner drummer trying to fit in. But they all watched and listened, nodding their heads to the beat. All the while I kept thinking, *Is this actually happening? Am I playing this song I've heard a thousand times for Steven Tyler himself?*

We all threw ourselves into the experience. We decided to go for it. What other choice did we have? And when everything was said and done, we did it! Because we were willing to put our own egos aside, we got to be a part of something much bigger than ourselves. We left that experience thinking, *Wow, I can't believe I just did that!* What an incredible memory.

I might have been the worst player in the whole camp, but who cares? I got to share the experience with people I respect, and I did the best I could, and I'll never forget that feeling.

Go where you have no business being. Try what you don't have the skills to try. Put yourself in a position where you're certain you'll be the worst one there. Then, just have the best time with it. You can have a mountain of excuses . . . or you can have fun.

Beware of Hometown Syndrome

When I came back from the Olympic Games with my gold medal in 1984, then-governor of Colorado Richard Lamm sat me down. He said, "Scott, I want to warn you about something I call hometown syndrome." It's something that happens to many athletes when they return from the big games and are worshipped for their achievements. It's easy to let all the attention go to your head. It's fun now. Enjoy your moment. But this will fade.

No matter how accomplished or important you think you are, nothing can shield you from the reality of being human. You are not invincible. You are not more important than anyone around you.

It was March 17, 1997—ten years into my touring with Stars on Ice—the day I was diagnosed with testicular cancer. And it was then that I realized, all at once, that I was getting this diagnosis almost exactly twenty years after losing my mom to cancer. It was devastating. But that day I did the same thing I did every day. I put on my skates and got on the ice and performed the show.

The next morning I woke up and started my adventure of getting my health back. Everything I had learned about being a champion—about fight and drive and what it meant to be a winner on the ice—I could use to fight the most important battle I had ever fought: the battle for my life.

When I started skating, I had no idea I would get cancer. I had no idea I would get involved with cancer research. And yet, looking back, I can see how all the moments of my life tied together to have a deeper purpose and meaning. My mom's death when I was very young propelled me into skating, motivated me to do the work it took to be a champion.

Then my own battle with cancer gave me empathy and a much greater understanding of everyone else who has to walk this road.

My successful skating career gave me access to people, resources, and opportunities I could use to help. And now, with the Scott Hamilton CARES Foundation, I get to play a key role in research, education, and survivorship for hundreds, even thousands, of people who have suffered like my mom and I have.

The great thing about finishing first is that it opens doors to new opportunities. It teaches you things you wouldn't have known otherwise. It gives people confidence in your ability to meet objectives and be successful. And ultimately it makes you the kind of person we all want to become.

What if I had stopped at the gold medal? What if I had

decided that was my greatest achievement and it was time to throw in the towel? Can you imagine what I would have missed? The opportunity to participate in one of the most rewarding, fulfilling, and important victories of my life.

I'm not trying to point the finger at myself and say I have it all figured out. I'm nobody special. I've made as many mistakes as the next person—probably more. All I'm saying is that we can't get caught up in our mistakes, our failures, our setbacks, or our victories. None of it defines us. None of this is worth holding on to. We have to build on every victory toward our next victory, or we'll miss the incredible potential we each have to bring our gifts to the world.

Don't Settle for Celebrity Status

I'm grateful that I get to meet people all the time who have every reason to boast in their successes but don't. Several years ago I was at a party and saw the front man for the band The Knack from across the room. You probably know them from their hit song "My Sharona." I couldn't believe it. He was someone I admired, and I knew he'd had some trouble with his health, so I went over to introduce myself. We ended up having a great conversation about life and health. Never once did he act like he was too important to talk to me.

Ringo Starr was at the same party. I walked over to him and said, "You're Ringo!" and have to admit I was a bit starstruck. Meanwhile he just sort of shrugged as if to say, "Yes, I am...."

True stars don't get too wrapped up in their accomplishments. They know what they achieved is just something they did. What's far more important is who they are.

You can tell the difference between celebrities and stars because true "stars" don't walk into a room flaunting their status. They are facing forward. Not resting in the past. They're wondering what comes next and what bigger impact they can make.

You can grasp the future, but you can't touch the past. So you cannot let your past define your future. The past is over. I'm not that kid who came in last in Novice Men anymore. I'm also not just an Olympic gold medalist. We are constantly evolving. Now on to new goals. Cancer research and serving the skating community. Dad to four. Husband to Tracie. What's past was past. I'm pointing myself toward the future.

Too many people in our world today settle for being celebrities—famous for not doing anything at all—and their characters reflect it. There is temporary popularity, and then there is longevity. You can chase either one. At the end of the day, one is full of empty promises, and the other one is built on something solid.

I don't know about you, but I don't want to be known simply for being known. If I am going to be known, I want to be known because I've done something that matters.

Something that makes a difference, even if it's in just one person's life. Something small but meaningful. I'd like to be remembered because I worked hard, mastered a skill, shared what I had with the world, and didn't hold back.

Get What You Want

You can have anything you want; you just can't have everything you want. So you have to decide what is truly important to you and go for it.

No holding back.

If you want to be the best guitar player in the world, you're going to miss out on some nights drinking with your friends. If you want to be a world-class juggling champion, you're probably not going to go on as many dates as the next guy. You do not have to worry about sacrificing too much. Balance is not something we have to seek. Balance achieves itself.

You may get started after a goal and realize you don't care about it as much as you thought you did. Maybe you thought you wanted to be a weight-lifting champion, but now you realize you really want to be a father. Maybe you thought you wanted to become chief executive officer of your company, but now you realize you actually want to volunteer at your church. Whatever you do, be the best at it. This is what finishing first is all about. Not making value judgments on what goals matter more than others. It's about discovering the limits of your human potential. Can you be the very best at whatever you decide to do?

There is a healthy balance of ambition and relationships, but most of us have not tipped the scales yet. The beautiful thing about balance is that anytime anything gets out of balance, it tends to reset itself. Our job is in learning to pay attention to these cues.

For me, the cancer diagnosis was the first time I realized the balance was off. Cancer brought things back into balance for me. I could have noticed sooner. But when the diagnosis came, I realized I couldn't ignore what was happening anymore. It was my wake-up call to slow down, take care of myself, and set a new course for life.

That journey was painful. At the same time, it was through this process that I discovered a new ambition—to have a healthy family. I realized I was actually more comfortable in front of seventeen thousand people than I was in front of one person, and I wanted that to change. And wouldn't you know—it wasn't too long after this that I met my wife.

You may worry that success is going to close doors. The truth is, it will. But it will open more doors than it closes. You earn a level of respect, a reputation. It sets you up on a firm foundation for everything else you want to do. Your problem is not that you have too much ambition but that you haven't tested the limits of your ambition yet. When you do, you'll find what you're capable of achieving.

Reinvent Your Success

I knew a guy many years ago who was not the most gifted skater. To do the jumps that came easily to everyone else, he had to break them down into smaller movements, picking the jump apart until he could teach himself all the little steps. Then he could string those steps together to perfect his jump.

He eventually became a competent skater but never a great skater. Do you know what he became instead? A great coach.

In fact, he became a brilliant coach. One of the best I've ever known. And part of what made him such a brilliant coach was that he knew how to break jumps into tiny little steps, to the point where he could pick apart a skater's jump and pinpoint exactly where the problem was. Then he could have the skater practice the problem area over and over again until the jump was flawless. What he thought was success for him turned out not to be success. And still, he is a champion. A world-class figure skating coach.

For every decade of your life, success looks different. That's okay.

It's more than okay, actually. It's normal. We always have an opportunity to reinvent ourselves. If you don't like who you are, ask yourself, "Okay, who's next?" Not "What's next?" but "Who is next?" In other words, "Who do I want to be in this next season?"

The most important work I will do in my life has nothing to do with skating and everything to do with spreading a message of hope to anyone who will listen. I'm not a celebrity. I'm not a hometown hero. I'm doing the work to build my future and have a pretty good idea where I'm trying to go. If you are ready to be done resting in what you've accomplished in the past, you can start today by dreaming about what is coming in the future. You can take the first step toward what is next.

If you're holding on to past successes because you're afraid you'll never succeed again, ask yourself this: What is it costing you? What is it costing our world? What is it costing humanity? The dreams and goals in your heart now are the inspiring stories of our future. But only if you let go of who you were and start taking steps toward who you are becoming.

Let Go of the Past

I tell people they'll know the day they've truly survived cancer because they'll get upset while sitting in traffic. They'll start sweating the small stuff again. It's a privilege to be able to sweat the small stuff in our lives—yet it's a privilege that we can lay down anytime we choose, without having to face a life-threatening illness. Anytime we want, we can decide to live life with an open hand instead of a clenched fist.

We all have things worth holding on to from our past, and we all have things we'd like to forget. I've made every mistake you can make. This is why I stay so focused on my faith in Jesus. Because of who He is, because of what He did, everything we are, everything we've done—it is all in the past. The future is made clean. His mercies are new every morning.

Shortly after my first brain tumor, I was baptized. As I was lowered into the water, I realized all the things that had happened in my past had led me to this moment. They had all led me here and yet I was getting to let go. It was a powerful moment I'll never forget.

My wife, Tracie, was putting our son Aidan into his car seat after everything had happened, and she looked up at me.

"How do you feel?" she asked. The only thing I could think to say was, "Lighter." All that stuff got me here, but I'm not going to carry it around anymore. Any of it. The success or the failure.

This, honestly, is my favorite thing about my faith. We have no right to hang on to anything anymore, except Jesus. It's been taken and paid for. It's time to move on. You can call us crazy, those of us who believe this, but pay attention. We're happier and lighter.

CHAPTER 12

WINNING CHANGES EVERYTHING

*Maybe the game of your life simply means
the one that most inspires other people.*

–TIM HOWARD[1]

What it looks like to finish first has changed everything for me over the years. Since I quit skating, I've fought and beat more than one brain tumor. My wife and I adopted two kids from Haiti, and now we have four children. I'm focused on being a dad now, and a good husband to Tracie, and my health, since the brain tumor returned last year. I'm focusing on cancer research, hoping we can change the way cancer is diagnosed and treated.

It's illogical what I've accomplished in my lifetime, illogical that I have even tried. I look back on it now and see how so many things could have just collapsed. It was all God. He allowed me to fail where He wanted me to fail so I could learn. And, at the same time, every single success was because of Him.

When people ask me about finishing first, that's the first thing I tell them—that if there is an "it" factor here, it can't be explained. It's like catching lightning in a bottle. It's not very probable. It's like I told the doctors at my most recent checkup for the brain tumor that has returned now three times. They kept looking at my scans, trying to figure out how it was possible that, in the latest scan, the tumor was smaller than it had been in the previous scan. That wasn't supposed to happen. It was so improbable.

When I was told that the tumor shrank, I asked the doctor how that was possible. He just smiled and said, "God."

Amazingly, miraculously, I am living a life that I never could have imagined. It doesn't make sense. And at the same time, I know it all makes perfect sense. Heavenly sense. God has always promised to do more than we would ever ask or imagine. It's just that so few of us take Him up on His offer.

I'm not done. I'm never done. In fact, I'm doing my most important winning work now. But everything I love about my life came from winning. Being a winner doesn't stop because I'm not in ice skates anymore.

God Will Wink

People talk all the time about "big breaks" when it comes to success. I don't think too much about big breaks, but I think the world of what my friend SQuire Rushnell would call "God winks." God winks are right-place-right-time situations. They are about trusting in a power greater than yourself that can help you win in a way you couldn't by yourself. This kind of winning has nothing to do with you, is bigger than you, and points you back to the purpose you're serving that is greater than yourself.

SQuire has had personal experience with this since writing a book years ago about God winks. He did what most authors do when they publish a book, which is to hit the ground running, trying to sell copies. Marketing. Publicity. The whole deal. Then one day Oprah was giving a televised tour of her house, and on her bedside table was a copy of SQuire's book. Talk about a God wink!

The next day sales for his book went through the roof. He had put in the work to write a great book. But that last little push he needed to find success came in a way he could not have arranged, even if he had tried.

SQuire had sent a copy of the book to me early on in the process, but I didn't get it because it accidentally went to an old address of mine in Los Angeles. Then one day I was sitting in Nashville, having lunch at a restaurant, and in walks SQuire with his wife. He just happened to be in Nashville for a day or two. He just happened to come into that restaurant. He just happened to come at the exact time I was there. So now he was able to send a copy of his book to my new address. Everything about our meeting that day was exactly what his book is about. That was a God wink.

The more we pay attention to God winks, the more we begin to find them everywhere we go. Whether you believe in God or not, if you begin to look for God winks, you'll find them.

Your Confidence Will Increase

You think you don't have enough confidence in yourself to become a champion? Try winning a little bit. See if that increases your confidence.

Find something you think you "can't" do and then do it anyway. Nothing will increase your faith in yourself like finishing first.

Like most men, I married out of my league. I'm not someone most women would look twice at. Yet my wife is beautiful in every way, talented, and the kindest woman you will ever meet. How did I ever get the opportunity to meet her, let alone have the confidence to talk to her?

I'm pretty sure it was the powder blue tights I was wearing the day I met her. Our mutual friend Tony Thomas had invited her to come see the show Stars on Ice, and my last solo was a ballet comedy I was doing that year. My name was Hamscott Tiltonovich (whatever it takes to get them on their feet!). Some people might have felt insecure meeting a romantic interest in powder blue tights, but whatever it was that made me appealing to her that day, she's still here.

Winning not only allows you to build confidence in

yourself, but it also creates confidence in others, in their image of you. It changes the way people interact with you, the way it changed how Tracie saw me that day. It builds a trust, which becomes a platform for you to do whatever else you want to do. Once you have a proven track record, people are much more likely to trust you with just about anything. Where you used to have to fight to earn trust, you don't have to fight so hard anymore.

Why would Target ask me to be their spokesperson for two Christmas holidays in a row—their biggest sales season? Because there was trust. My reputation preceded me and they trusted that I would represent them well. How was I able to do nine Disney television specials? All of these opportunities were offshoots of one decision to win.

If I had come in ninth in Nationals the year I won, I never would have met my wife. I cringe to think how different my life would be if I had missed even one of those wins. I never would be in the position to be doing the kind of work I'm doing today. I wouldn't have the marriage I have, the family I have, the life I have, the financial security I have. One win leads to another win leads to another win.

Not to mention, I never would have been able to do all that I've done for cancer research. At the end of the day, who cares what I did for competitive skating? If I can accomplish what I know is possible in the world of cancer, I'll know why I'm here. I'll have found my purpose.

This is what finishing first is all about—breaking through limitations and barriers, discovering your deepest purpose, and making the biggest impact in the world that you are capable of. As long as you are always reaching for greater depth, greater meaning, greater results, you'll never be bored. And pretty soon, if you keep going, it won't even be about you anymore. It will be about something so much bigger and better.

When you start to see what a positive impact winning can have in your life, you stop giving yourself permission to falter. You stop making excuses. You stop worrying about what people are going to say or what they are going to think. You finally take the leap you've been wanting to take, needing to take. You start to be the kind of person who finishes first.

Your Desires Will Shift

When I was at the top of my professional career, I was on top of the world, but I was also missing something. Being on the road all the time makes it hard to have any consistency in your life, any real relationships. You become close, in a way, with the people traveling with you, but, otherwise, most of the people you see are strangers. Here one day, gone the next.

When I met Tracie, that changed, but it wasn't really until my first son, Aidan, was born that I realized I needed to pivot my definition of success, of finishing first. I needed to adjust my priorities, to come off the road. I always half joke that as far as professional skating was concerned, I milked that cow dry. This is one way you can know when it's time to pivot—when there's no milk left in the cow.

There's something so basic about the pursuit of material success—money, fame, awards, promotions. I don't know anyone who hasn't, at some point in his or her life, at least had the desire to go after these things. In fact, I would argue that this is all part of the process, part of finishing first. How can we be better tomorrow than we are today? What is the next level of success, and how can I get there?

At the same time, there comes a point in your life when you realize that the things you really want to "win" at now are different than they were in the beginning. When being the best husband you could possibly be fills the place of standing on a podium. When getting your kids on their feet about something like Disney World feels better than getting a stadium of strangers on their feet.

And the shift doesn't have to be a big dramatic thing, either.

Sometimes you shift from one career to another career. Maybe you shift from career to relationship, or relationship to career. I shifted to being at home more often and off the road, but I also shifted in this phase of my life to being an author and a speaker. I shifted to doing television broadcasting.

People sometimes wonder when it's time to pivot away from one area of success and focus on another, and the truth is that often it's obvious.

Sometimes life does the shifting for you. You lose someone you love. You go through a divorce. You have a baby. But if you still need help knowing for sure, I always say a good gauge is when your level of satisfaction has diminished.

I knew it was time for me to stop when the great shows didn't feel as great as the bad shows felt bad. That's when I could say, "Okay, the scales have tipped. It's time to look toward the next thing." The thing that had always brought me so much joy before wasn't bringing me the same level of joy, and that's when I realized my heart had shifted to a new place. As soon as Aidan came on the scene, it was like, "Check, please."

The thing I started to see was that once you start a family, you can only be as successful in your life as you are in your family. If your family suffers, everything else suffers with it. And so, for me, there has been no greater joy than finishing first in the context of my family.

If you're driven to succeed, you may also find there is no greater challenge than finishing first with your family. Use this as your very reason to do it well. Make this your next marker of success. How can you be better than you've ever been for your spouse and your children? How can you be the best you've ever been in your relationships? Become successful where you've never been successful before—at home.

It's also possible that you're reading this book and you're single. You might be wondering when that time will come for you. If this is you, I want to say to you how grateful I am that I leveraged the time before I had a family to finish first in my career. I was forty-four when I got married, and it was the right time for me. Not too early. Not too late. Exactly the right time. So if you're wondering if it is "too late" for you, I would tell you there is no such thing. Stay on your path. The time will come for you, and when it does, it will change everything.

How you participate in your family situation is an extension of where you are as a person. You cannot be for your family someone you aren't, period. Who you are becoming now will play a role in the kind of husband or wife you will be, the kind of mother or father you will be. Are you fully formed? Are you able to overcome failures? Are you the kind of person who does what you say you are going to do? Who works hard? Who keeps showing up?

Finishing first will make you the strongest, most resilient you you've ever been. Later, your family will thank you for it.

The World You Move in Will Change

We can skip all the drama and heartache that comes along with finishing first if we want to. We can skip the failure and the pain of failing. We can just sit on our couches and watch television. But what would we miss?

When I look back at the life I've lived so far, I see a lot of pain. I failed constantly. But I learned from each of those failures, and none of my success would have been possible without them. They're all connected.

My coach used to say whenever I complained about being in pain, "The absence of pain is death." And he's right. Imagine if we didn't feel pain. Consider if we didn't have any suffering in our lives. How shallow would life be? Sure, we'd avoid that temporary uncomfortable feeling, but we'd also miss the amazing feeling of overcoming. The realization that we are so much stronger than we think.

Most of us forget that the very things that seem to be working against us are actually working for us, if we're willing to see them that way. My life has been a series of accidents and setbacks that have all led me to where I am. The whole reason I succeeded in skating was because my life didn't go at all the way I wanted it to.

If we never ran the marathon, we'd never get to cross the finish line. Someone could take you to the finish line of a marathon and let you step across the line, but it wouldn't mean much to you. But once you've run that marathon? Once you've suffered every excruciating step? Suddenly, stepping across the finish line is one of the greatest victories of your life.

I don't know about you, but when I get to the end of my life, I want to be able to feel like I gave it everything I had. I left it all on the field. I pushed myself to the very limits of my human capacity. And as long as I'm here, I never want to be finished dreaming and pushing myself.

The most amazing thing about success is that it builds on itself. Once you hit a critical mass, things start happening in a new way. Each little victory builds on the last and you start to experience the most amazing momentum. It's motivating to keep pushing, keep stretching, keep reaching for the next thing. How can we be the kind of people who are constantly raising the bar?

At some point we all have to make a decision about what kind of life we're going to lead. Are we going to keep letting our fears, doubts, egos, and critics hold us back? Or are we done being that person and ready to be the person who shrugs it all off and says, "I'm going for this anyway"? Hebrews 12:1 says, "Therefore, since we are surrounded by such a great cloud of witnesses, let us throw off everything that hinders and the sin that so easily entangles. And let us run with perseverance the race marked out for us."

Leaving everything behind and moving forward is the healthiest, best, strongest way to get to where you want to be.

Think about if you never took a chance. What if, at the end of your days, you looked back and saw nothing but squandered opportunity? How devastating would that be? All that is in front of you is more love, more happiness, more success, more joy than you've ever experienced before. That is, if you're willing to constantly push the limits. Constantly raise the bar. Constantly make this world a better place for us and for our children.

Why would you ever dare to finish first? Why would you put in all the work, put in all the effort, take the risk, put yourself on the line? Because winning changes everything. It changes you—how you carry yourself, what you can and can't accomplish, the opportunities available to you, and the amount of beauty you're able to bring to the world. It also changes everyone around you. Winning raises the bar. It makes everyone better. It makes the world a better place.

The kind of world I want to live in is a world where nobody is settling for what they were capable of yesterday. A world where people are breaking barriers and overcoming the "limits" that have been placed on them and where we are all proving that anything is possible with faith, hard work, and dedication. To me, that is a much happier, more compelling world than the one where we hand out ninth-place trophies and participation ribbons.

What are you waiting for?

WINS COME IN ALL SHAPES AND SIZES

When I was diagnosed with cancer in 1997, I realized this was the biggest competition of my life. I was on unfamiliar ground, meaning I didn't know anything about cancer or chemo or surgery or how to beat this disease. But at the same time, I realized I knew exactly what to do because I had been training for this moment my entire life. Everything I had learned about winning and losing and fighting and becoming a champion would now inform how I faced this new challenge. There was only once choice: to win. That decision was literally life or death.

I'm so grateful for what I've learned about uncovering my greatest potential, not only because it has earned me all of the most beautiful experiences of my life this far but also because it saved my life.

In writing this book, I meant for it to be broad in its application. By that I mean that even if you don't consider yourself an athlete or you don't see yourself as a particularly competitive person, I wanted the stories I told you here to motivate you to *live*—whatever that means for you. This is more than sports. It's more than business. It's more than family. It's more than personal ambitions. This book is meant to give you the fortitude to rise above whatever challenge is in your way. Once you know how to do this, you'll be prepared for anything.

It occurred to me that perhaps you've made it this far in the book and you're still wondering, "What am I going to *do*?" In which case, I wanted to see if I could give you some practical help for getting started with your version of finishing first.

How to Get Started

People often ask me how they should know where to start. For some people this stems from a lack of ideas. For others, it stems from *too many* ideas. They want to know which one to pick first. Regardless of which one sounds like you, my suggestion is the same: start with something you've been putting off forever. You know what I mean—that nagging feeling that something is unfinished. We have a thousand reasons we never get started with these projects, but what if you pushed aside your excuses and got going?

This doesn't have to be special or profound. You can start by going to visit that friend or picking up the phone and calling a family member with whom you've been out of touch. You could read the book that's been sitting on your shelf for months, or you could finally sign up for that dance class. Go bowling, write a poem, make homemade bread—whatever is in your heart. Just find *something* you've been putting on the back burner and give yourself permission to do it.

My family moved into the house we're living in seven years ago, and ever since then, I've been meaning to clean out the garage. You know how this goes. It always gets scheduled for some time in the distant future and then gets pushed back because some other "emergency" comes up. In fact, if it weren't that with every rain and every time a car gets parked in the garage the condensation builds, and it's beyond hazardous, I probably never would have gotten around to it.

But thankfully, since I am interested in avoiding my wife needing a total hip replacement, I decided one Saturday to just bite the bullet and do it. Of course it was inconvenient. Of course there were a thousand other things I could think of doing on a Saturday. Of course I thought about putting it off again. And, at the same time, we sometimes exert far more effort avoiding something than we would if we would just get over ourselves and get it done.

So I got out there one Saturday and put in the work. I organized and purged and cleaned and made space. Once I got into it, I realized it wasn't that hard and wondered why it had taken me so long to get started. Then, when everything was done, I came back in the house in the late afternoon and had that familiar feeling that makes all the effort worth it. It's like, "Victory!" We finished something. We let go of all of our excuses. We got off the couch and accomplished something we've wanted to do for such a long time.

The thing with finishing something is it creates space. It opens up room. So now you can move on to the next thing, something perhaps that's more fun or more exciting or that you want to do more than cleaning out the garage. There's something to say for building momentum. The first thing on your list doesn't have to be profound. In fact, if you start with the easiest thing on your list, you're 100 percent more likely to actually get it done.

And when that's out of the way—out of your mental and emotional space—what will you do with the room that's opened up? What is the next idea or dream you'll chase?

Finish First—For You

Of the seven billion people on the planet, no two are the same. Which means winning, for you, will be as unique as *you* are. There is no right or wrong way to do this. There are no rules. If being successful in business doesn't sound that interesting to you, then don't do it! If making money doesn't make your heart leap a little, then leave that ambition for someone else. If writing poetry sounds like a drag, then that doesn't have to be the way you finish first.

What is it that would make *you* feel like you've fulfilled your purpose on this planet? This is your story to write, your victory to have. These are your ambitions to pursue. I'm not interested in helping everyone win an Olympic gold medal. That's *my* story. It doesn't have to be yours. I'm interested in helping you uncover the joy and meaning that's found in you becoming a better version of you than you ever dreamed you could be.

This is not just about having a goal. It's about how having a goal permeates every part of your life. It's about having ambitions that strengthen who *you* are as a person. And for each and every one of us to reach the pinnacle of our now unique purpose—it will not only change your individual world, but it will also change the world itself.

How Faith Plays a Role

Over the 2017 Memorial Day weekend, right after I finished writing this book, something happened. I went from playing UNO with my son one night to waking up the next morning with every neurological symptom you can imagine. I was going in and out of consciousness, and time was jumping. Almost the feeling you get when you wake up and then close your eyes for a second, but really two hours have passed. I'd be sitting there looking at my wife, and I'd feel myself starting to go away. Then, all of a sudden, I'd be back.

I took an ambulance ride to Vanderbilt University Medical

Center and was admitted immediately to neurological ICU. I suddenly realized this might be it. The end. And you know what? I was okay with it. I was at peace. When I thought back on my life, I realized I had no regrets, that I had done what I came here to do. That's actually an amazing feeling—when you come to the end of everything and realize it's all going to be okay.

The doctors kept asking me how I was feeling, and I told them I was seeing double or triple. Only one doctor would be standing there, but I would see two or three. Then I would try to reach up my hand to scratch my head, but my hand would flop around. I had no motor ability whatsoever.

The doctors checked all of the obvious concerns. My white count was stable, and I had no fever. They scanned the tumor, and it was the same size it had always been. My symptoms had come on all at once, and they couldn't figure out what it meant. If my body was a battery, I felt like I was down to 1 percent.

Tracie came over to check on me, and I was still moving in and out of consciousness but decided it was probably time to give her my last words. So I started telling her the things I wanted her to know, and what I wanted our kids to know, before it was all over. We prayed together. We said the Lord's Prayer several times and prayed for God's power, the love and healing of Jesus Christ. We prayed for it all. And then, again, I drifted off.

Two hours later I woke up and saw Tracie there, in the same place she had been standing when I fell asleep.

"Are you okay?" I heard her ask.

I thought about it for a moment. Scanned my body. Took a deep breath. Then I looked at her and said resolutely, "Actually, yeah—I feel *a lot* better."

Having survived that little setback, I've been reminded—in a number of ways—that the bodies we've been given are temporary. They are extremely fragile but hold the capacity to be incredibly resilient. Every day is not just a gift but an *opportunity*. On my fiftieth birthday, when I thought about my mother and realized she died at forty-nine, I reminded myself once again that I need to do something that matters in the second half of my life. Life is temporary and fragile. But we are phenomenally powerful and resilient.

What do you want to do with your life—wherever you are in it?

While we're here, it is my belief that we are responsible to do as much good as possible. There is so much goodness in you that has yet to be discovered. So much beauty that is still unfolding. What are some things you've been wanting to do but have been putting off? I'm hoping that the words in this book will inspire you to live those dreams, those goals, those desires with greater joy in the challenge. Go get 'em.

When You Get to Say "I Win"

I'm sure your life hasn't been easy. We all have challenges we face. These things happen, I believe, so that we see God's hand in it. So that when He moves, as He always does, we can point to that as a reminder of how powerful He is and how much He loves us. It's not an easy road, but when we cling closely to Him, He reveals Himself to us and to the world around us.

Winning, ultimately, has everything to do with Him and nothing to do with us. The glory is all His.

On October 29, 1997, six and a half months after my first cancer diagnosis, chemotherapy, and surgery, I gave a comeback show at the Forum in Los Angeles. After I finished my performance, which was physically and emotionally taxing, they handed me a microphone. They wanted to know my thoughts. I was silent for a moment. Longer than normal. And then, when I finally spoke up, I spoke clearly and resolutely.

The first two words were: *I win*.

ACKNOWLEDGMENTS

Finish First would not have been possible without the support of these very special people.

My wife, Tracie—you saved me from myself and allowed me to understand what true love is, and how beautiful it is to serve those in great need.

My children, Aidan, Maxx, Jean Paul, and Evelyne—my greatest blessings. You inspire me every day and have shown me the meaning of limitless, unconditional love.

I love you five forever!

My coach, Don Laws—I am grateful beyond words for your dedication and guidance. Together we won four US Championships, four World Championships, and an Olympic gold medal: 17–0. I still can't believe it. We will have eternity to reminisce in heaven!

My friend, Donald Miller—you inspired the creation of this book. Your humor and kind, intelligent heart are gifts to me and to this world.

ACKNOWLEDGMENTS

Ally Fallon—thank you for sharing this journey with me. I wouldn't have wanted to create this book with anyone else.

Wes Yoder—thank you for representing this project. I am very grateful that this book introduced me to you. Here's to years of friendship.

Debbie Wickwire—your strength and faith without limit and your endless support. Thank you for always believing in me.

A special thank you to every single person who has defeated me. Whether it was in skating, business, or on a personal level, you helped shape the life I enjoy today.

NOTES

Chapter 1: Why You Aren't a Winner—Yet

1. "Famous Quotes by Vince Lombardi," Results/Winning, Vince Lombardi, accessed August 14, 2017, www.vincelombardi.com /quotes.html.

Chapter 2: Know Your Purpose

1. Leo Rosten, as quoted in the *Sunday Star*, newspaper of Washington, DC, from his 1962 address. This quote is often attributed to Ralph Waldo Emerson.

Chapter 3: Break the Pattern of Losing

1. Samuel Smiles, *Self-Help* (New York: London, Harper & Brothers, 1900), 212.

Chapter 4: Commit to the Long Haul

1. Robert Collier, *Riches Within Your Reach* (New York: Penguin, 2009).
2. *Heads and Tales at Marin Academy*; "The Necessity of Stress," blog entry, December 12, 2013, https://travisma.wordpress .com/2013/12/12/the-necessity-of-stress/.

Chapter 5: Keep Showing Up

1. Emmitt Smith, as quoted in Wayne Mazzoni, *You vs. You: Sport Psychology for Life* (Mazz Marketing Inc, 2005).

Chapter 6: Overcome Your Limitations

1. Henry Ford, quoted in Erika Anderson, "21 Quotes from Henry Ford on Business, Leadership, and Life," *Forbes*, May 31, 2013, https://www.forbes.com/sites/erikaandersen/2013/05/31/21 -quotes-from-henry-ford-on-business-leadership-and-life /#53e1d2c293c5.
2. "Kyle Maynard: No Arms and No Legs Climbing Mount Kilimanjaro," YouTube video, 11:20, posted by Mark Heninger, May 2, 2013, see :00:42, https://m.youtube.com /watch?v=LuH4sK25AwE.

Chapter 7: Outwork Everyone

1. Bobby Knight, quoted in Luke Kerr-Dineen, "The 48 Greatest Quotes About Winning," *USA Today*, February 9, 2016, http:// ftw.usatoday.com/2016/02/best-sports-quotes-about-winning.

Chapter 8: Ditch Fear and Celebrate Failure

1. Theodore Roosevelt, quoted in William Safire, *Lend Me Your Ears: Great Speeches of History* (New York: W. W. Norton, 2004).

Chapter 9: Edit Your Critics

1. Chuck Noll, quoted in "Ron Cook: For Noll, Joy's Soul Lay in the Doing," *Pittsburgh Post-Gazette*, June 14, 2014, http://www.post-gazette.com/sports/2014/06/15/Ron-Cook -For-Noll-joy-s-soul-lay-in-the-doing/stories/201406150214.
2. Roy F. Baumeister, et al., "Bad Is Stronger Than Good," *Review of General Psychology*, 5, no. 4 (2001): 323–70, http://assets.csom .umn.edu/assets/71516.pdf.

Chapter 10: Play by the Rules of the Game

1. Helen Keller, quoted in Lana Tracy Lewis, *Living Life Consciously* (Bloomington, IN: AuthorHouse, 2009), 133.

Chapter 11: Never Look Back

1. Pat Summitt, quoted in Jeff Haden, "300 Motivational Quotes to Help You Achieve Your Dreams," Inc.com, December 15, 2015, https://www.inc.com/jeff-haden/300-motivational-quotes-to-inspire-you-to-achieve-your-dreams.html.

Chapter 12: Winning Changes Everything

1. Tim Howard, *The Keeper, Young Reader's Edition: The Unguarded Story of Tim Howard* (New York: Harper, 2014).

ABOUT THE AUTHOR

Scott Hamilton is a living example of good guys who finish first. He is a *New York Times* bestselling author, Olympic champion, cancer survivor, broadcaster, motivational speaker, author, husband, father, eternal optimist, and firm believer that the only disability in life is a bad attitude. For more than twenty years, Scott has inspired audiences around the world with the story of his life and how he has overcome adversities. He lives near Nashville with his beautiful wife, Tracie, and their four amazing children.

"Scott Hamilton . . . lives his life as a champion. Everyone needs the positive message of this greatly inspiring book."

–Kristi Yamaguchi, Olympic Gold Medalist

"I know and love Scotty Hamilton. You will, too, after you read this book."

–William Shatner

"It's like my bud Scott says, 'You can't just skate through life and expect to be happy!'"

–Kevin Nealon, actor, comedian, *Saturday Night Live* alum

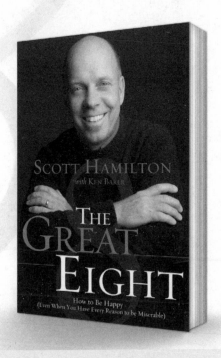

From Gold Medalist to cancer and brain tumor survivor, Scott Hamilton has experienced the heights of accomplishment to the depths of disease. But through his successes, struggles, and setbacks, Hamilton has never lost his trademark humor and honesty. But more important, he has never lost his faith and optimism. How *does* he keep smiling?

In *The Great Eight*, Scott uses stories from his international career and personal life to describe the eight secrets that—through commitment and repetition—have helped him "clear the ice," get back up, and "smile like Kristi Yamaguchi."